ORTHO'S All About

Tiling Basics

Meredith® Books
Des Moines, Iowa

Ortho® Books
An imprint of Meredith® Books

All About Tiling Basics
Editor: Larry Johnston
Art Director: Tom Wegner
Assistant Art Director: Harijs Priekulis
Copy Chief: Catherine Hamrick
Copy and Production Editor: Terri Fredrickson
Book Production Managers: Pam Kvitne,
 Marjorie J. Schenkelberg
Contributing Copy Editor: Steve Hallam
Technical Proofreader: Pete Bird
Contributing Proofreaders: Dan J. Degen,
 Debra Morris Smith, Beth Lastine
Electronic Production Coordinator: Paula Forest
Editorial and Design Assistants: Kathleen Stevens,
 Karen Schirm

**Additional Editorial Contributions from
 Greenleaf Publishing**
Publishing Director: Dave Toht
Writers: Steve Cory and Dave Toht
Copy Editor: Barbara Webb
Art Director: Jean DeVaty
Designer: Melanie Lawson, Melanie Lawson Design
Associate Designer: Rebecca JonMichaels
Illustrators: Tony Davis, Jonathan Clark
Additional Photography: Dan Stultz
Technical Consultant: Ray Allred
Indexer: Nan Badgett

Meredith® Books
Editor in Chief: James D. Blume
Design Director: Matt Strelecki
Managing Editor: Gregory H. Kayko
Executive Ortho Editor: Larry Erickson

Director, Retail Sales and Marketing: Terry Unsworth
Director, Sales, Special Markets: Rita McMullen
Director, Sales, Premiums: Michael A. Peterson
Director, Sales, Retail: Tom Wierzbicki
Director, Sales, Home & Garden Centers: Ray Wolf
Director, Book Marketing: Brad Elmitt
Director, Operations: George A. Susral
Director, Production: Douglas M. Johnston

Vice President, General Manager: Jamie L. Martin

Meredith Publishing Group
President, Publishing Group: Christopher M. Little
Vice President, Finance & Administration: Max Runciman

Meredith Corporation
Chairman and Chief Executive Officer: William T. Kerr

Chairman of the Executive Committee: E.T. Meredith III

Thanks to
Armor Tile Supply, Crestwood, Ill.
Katie Usedom, Designing Dishes, Geneva, Ill.

Photographers
(Photographers credited may retain copyright ©
 to the listed photographs.)
Rick Taylor: Cover
Dan Stultz: 3, 20, 22–33, 37, 41, 43, 46, 49–53, 55, 56, 59,
 68, 70, 71, 82, 88, 90, 91

All of us at Ortho® Books are dedicated to providing you
with the information and ideas you need to enhance your
home and garden. We welcome your comments and
suggestions about this book. Write to us at:
 Meredith Corporation
 Ortho Books
 1716 Locust St.
 Des Moines, IA 50309–3023

If you would like more information on other Ortho
products, call 800-225-2883 or visit us at www.ortho.com

Note to the Readers: Due to differing conditions, tools,
and individual skills, Meredith Corporation assumes no
responsibility for any damages, injuries suffered, or losses
incurred as a result of following the information published
in this book. Before beginning any project, review the
instructions carefully, and if any doubts or questions remain,
consult local experts or authorities. Because codes and
regulations vary greatly, you always should check with
authorities to ensure that your project complies with all
applicable local codes and regulations. Always read and
observe all of the safety precautions provided by
manufacturers of any tools, equipment, or supplies,
and follow all accepted safety procedures.

DESIGNING & DECORATING WITH TILE 4

CHOOSING TILE & GROUT 20

TILING PREPARATION 32

INSTALLING TILE 50

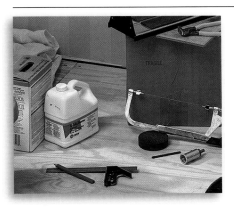

REPAIRS & MAINTENANCE 88

This inviting room is a study in earth tones. Large slate tiles of various colors surround the fireplace and extend to the ceiling. The clay tile on the floor (well sealed so it is easy to keep clean) is less dramatic in color, providing a calm background that ties together the furnishings and woodwork.

DESIGNING & DECORATING WITH TILE

Durable and colorful, by turns exciting and calming—ceramic tile has brought color and texture to surfaces for thousands of years. Yet it is as contemporary as any hot new product.

Throughout these pages, you will find tile installations and color combinations to kick-start your imagination as you decide how to bring tile into your home. In addition to ceramic tile, you will see natural products such as marble, slate, and granite, as well as porcelain.

Expect to find decorating ideas almost anywhere: Check magazines and tile showrooms, of course, but also look around when in other people's homes or in buildings where you work or shop.

Many people assume that ceramic tile installation should be left to professionals. But if you are reasonably handy, have the patience to lay out the job carefully, and are prepared for some hard and gritty work, tiling is well within your reach. This book will guide you through all the steps.

This chapter explains basic design principles and describes the specific benefits of tile for various rooms in your home. Chapter two covers the variety of available materials. In chapter three, you'll learn about the all-important task of preparing surfaces for tiling. Chapter four leads you through the job of tiling. Finally, chapter five provides information about repairing damaged tile and some tips on maintaining tile surfaces.

THE BENEFITS OF TILE

Tile and stone are usually easy to maintain. Routine cleaning of glazed tile often requires little more than a quick sweep or a wipe with a damp mop or sponge. Even glazed tile that has suffered long neglect can be revived to a lustrous sheen with a good washing. However, some porous tile, such as marble or quarry tile, stains easily and can be difficult to clean.

Tile is remarkably durable. Ceramic tile installed in Egypt in 4700 B.C. retains its beauty to this day.

Tile acts as an efficient solar collector, too. In the winter, it stores heat during the day and slowly radiates it at night. In the summer, it absorbs warmth, diffusing the intensity of the sun's heat.

Tile offers excellent value. In many cases, ceramic tile costs about the same as vinyl flooring. And while tiling a wall costs more than painting or hanging wallpaper, it is far more durable in locations that get wet. Ceramic tile installation usually adds value to your home should you decide to sell it.

Salmon-colored tiles with sand-colored grout provide a functional and elegant setting for an outdoor spa. Ornamental trees and flowers flourish in tile-wrapped planting areas.

Continuing the same floor tile from the kitchen into the living room adds to the open look of the layout. An Oriental rug, combined with casual furniture, adds warmth and eases the utilitarian aspect of the floor.

Large black and green tiles over the range have designs featuring leaves and chrysanthemums to complement the wood tones in this kitchen.

Above: Tile is ideal for sunrooms with lots of indoor plants. Squares of blue-and-green mosaic tile set on point add detail to this floor of 12-inch clay tiles.

The tiled surround on this spa/tub features stunning cream-colored marble tiles. It also provides plenty of shelf space for flowers, candles, and decorative bath items.

TILE IN THE BATHROOM

Like a well-made brass faucet set, tile combines utility with timeless good looks. Because most bathrooms work hard every day, it makes sense to cover floors and walls with a durable material. Tile can easily withstand the splashed water, steam, and lingering humidity of a bathroom year after year. And it is easy to clean.

When planning your bathroom, choose glazed tiles, which do not absorb water, or apply enough sealer to unglazed tiles so that water beads up. If you install glazed tiles, you should seal the grout.

On the floor, lay glazed tiles with a matte finish or a texture for slip resistance. Or install mosaic tiles—the additional grouted joints between these tiles can make a nearly slip-free surface.

If possible, choose the whole ensemble at the same time—tiles, toilet, sink, tub or shower, plumbing fittings, and accessories such as soap dishes and towel racks to achieve a unified look. Stores that specialize in kitchen and bath materials might offer fixtures and tiles that match in color, but remember that some contrast and variety is desirable.

A glass corner shower shows off green, cream, and brown slate tiles on both floor and wall.

Rose-colored marble surrounds this spa. Grout between the white floor tiles matches one of the hues in the marble. Note the rhythm here: white floor tiles, rose vertical tiles, white spa, rose backsplash, and white window trim.

Tile covers the floor and three walls around the bathtub in a typical bathroom. But consider adding tile elsewhere. For instance, you can tile a tub or spa surround, then tile the sink top to match. Tiled windowsills withstand condensation and provide an ideal place to display potted plants.

If the colors are not overpowering, you can tile whole walls in a bathroom. You can even tile a ceiling. (However, consider hiring a pro for this difficult job. Tiles will adhere to the mastic surprisingly well, but matching up the ceiling grout lines with those of the wall tile can be very difficult.)

Traditionally, bathroom tiles are small—either 4 inches square or smaller. Larger tiles are harder to fit around the many obstructions in a bath and tend to look odd in small spaces. However, don't be afraid to lay large tiles on a broad expanse of floor or wall.

When planning your tiling job, consider a lighting upgrade. Take advantage of lighting to emphasize the beauty of tile, but avoid creating a glare. Track lighting, for instance, allows you to redirect lights for the best effect after installation.

Taupe-colored marble forms a step leading to the tub and another leading to the window for an elevated effect. Strong natural light from a large window enhances the spaciousness.

Twelve-inch white porcelain tiles look like marble but do not have to be sealed. The effect is clean and simple, but far from plain.

Set in an overlapping bricklike pattern, handsome marble tiles lend timelessness to this small bathroom.

TILE IN THE KITCHEN

Alternating green and white porcelain tiles lend a homey feel that is reminiscent of the 1950s without feeling old-fashioned.

The kitchen is often the heart of the home, where you spend hours cooking and cleaning, where your family meets several times a day, and where party goers often gravitate. Make it a warm and inviting place with decorative tile. Of course, tile also stands up to the steam, grease, and spattering that kitchen walls endure. And it can be wiped clean in a flash.

An often-debated point is: Should you install ceramic tile on a kitchen floor? Many homeowners prefer sheet vinyl or wood because they find tile too hard and believe a ceramic tile floor would be uncomfortable to stand on for hours at a time. In addition, a glass or plate dropped on a tile floor is likely to break; other surfaces might be more forgiving. These points are worth considering, but bear in mind that throw rugs (most kitchens have one) alleviate both problems. In the end, the advantages of decorative flexibility and durability outweigh the drawbacks of ceramic tile for many homeowners.

The wall between the countertop and a wall-hung cabinet is an excellent location for

This kitchen makes ample use of tile, combining dark patterned tiles, plain, cream-colored tiles, and rough slate on the floor.

ceramic tile. The area is just the right size—usually about 18 inches high—for a decorative strip that contrasts with cabinets and walls. And as an extended backsplash, it shines: Errant splashes of olive oil, flour, or cake batter quickly wipe away.

Tiled countertops receive mixed reviews; that's largely because inadequately sealed grout lines are difficult to keep clean. But if you apply grout sealer periodically, a tiled top will not be porous and will not harbor mildew. Following that simple maintenance step will allow you to enjoy a one-of-a-kind tile countertop that makes a dramatic contribution to your decor. The same pattern often can be used for the countertop and the backsplash. Special trim tiles designed specifically for countertops make layout and installation as easy as any other tile job.

Tile is ideal for the backsplash area above kitchen counters and offers plenty of options for decorative detailing.

Counters and walls covered with green porcelain tile provide a welcome splash of bright color to an otherwise austere kitchen.

TILE IN LIVING AREAS

Tile adds distinction and charm to any room of the house. It is usually less expensive than hardwood flooring and will cost less in the long run than wall-to-wall carpeting. Often, tile is combined with hardwood or carpeting to cover high-traffic areas—and provide variety to the decor.

An entryway provides a natural setting for a tile floor, one that mops up easily in wet or icy weather. The tile floor's strong grid pattern adds impact to a lackluster entryway, too. And because the floor area is usually small, you can splurge on stylish materials. Be sure to choose tiles that won't be slippery when wet.

Floor tile also proves a logical choice for a family room; food spills, crushed crayons, and pet accidents all clean up with ease.

Small sections of tile can add variety and unusual color to any living area. Fireplace surrounds and hearths, countertops, tabletops, and trim around windows all present enticing possibilities.

Informal living areas with easy access to the outdoors are logical areas for a tile floor.

Bright blue wall tiles highlight the fireplace and bring a splash of color to this room.

Tile takes a lot of punishment and is ideal for indoor gardening areas, especially those doubling as mudrooms. Tile also has the advantage of moderating temperature, radiating heat in the cool of the night, and slowing heat buildup on sunny days.

The pattern made by accent and border tiles on this floor mimics the patterns seen in Native American rugs.

Decorative tiles covering these stair risers combine beauty and utility.

TILE OUTDOORS

Tile on a patio, around a pool, or as a decorative element on outdoor stairs will refine outdoor living spaces, helping create clean, smooth surfaces for lounging, playing, and entertaining.

Many people assume that a patio must be built of rough materials like concrete pavers, bricks, or poured concrete. A properly installed tiled surface will be as durable. Laying the tiles is no more work than installing other paving materials, but you do need a solid concrete slab underneath. If you live in an area with cold winters, select a tile that will stand up to freeze/thaw cycles. Often, the same tile can serve indoors and outdoors. If you do a lot of outdoor dining, you might want to tile from the kitchen onto the patio with the same pattern.

In most cases, subdued color looks best—and pleases longest—on outdoor tiles. Earth tones, grays, and gentle greens show off potted plants better. However, you can add brightly colored tiles sparingly, as a border or randomly sprinkled throughout a field of tiles.

Unglazed clay tiles cut the glare but may not withstand severe winters; consult with your dealer for the right product. Small, hand-painted tiles help break up the grid.

These light gray tiles provide a complementary backdrop for potted plants and shrubs. Here, the same tile covers the horizontal and vertical surfaces and the stairs.

Irregularly shaped slate looks like flagstone but is smoother and easier to clean. It's an ideal indoor/outdoor flooring material.

Above: The varied colors and rough texture of slate tiles turn the patio into an eye-catching feature that complements the landscape. The same tile works equally well on stair risers, on stair treads, and as facing for the planters.

Glazed black tiles contrast starkly but pleasantly with the brick pavers surrounding this pool.

DESIGNING WITH COLOR

Color sets a mood, subtly influencing how people think and feel. So don't be surprised if you need to spend a lot of time choosing your tile colors.

Avoid choosing a tile color to match your walls or fabrics, because tile will last longer than other elements of the decor. When possible, choose tiles first, then select furnishings to harmonize.

Using all one color—or tiles with only slight variations in color—provides a neutral background that lets other elements of the decor shine through. Multiple colors can be exciting, but too many look busy and may become tiresome. Setting a few splashes of exciting color into a neutral background often is the best approach.

Look to nature for color combinations that at first may seem unlikely, but actually harmonize. A bed of flowers, for instance, may combine green, pink, orange, and yellow without being outlandish. Often the trick is getting just the right shade of the brighter colors.

The countertop and backsplash in this kitchen mix bright blue and white tiles in reversed patterns—lots of white for the backsplash, and lots of blue for the counter. Thin, copper-colored border tiles add depth to the color palette.

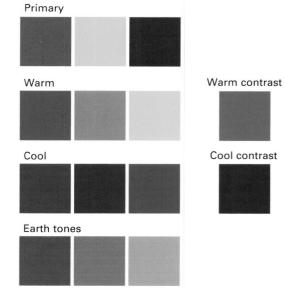

Primary

Warm

Warm contrast

Cool

Cool contrast

Earth tones

Variations of primary colors combine for a warm or cool effect. Select contrasting colors as accents. A base of neutral earth tones fits into a variety of decorating schemes.

Aggregations of mosaic tiles—the same size as the white tiles surrounding them—add spots of color. A dark border along the wall tiles sets off the random design.

Below: A small feature like this window seat is an ideal way to bring in a bold splash of color that accents the rest of the decor.

These unusual diamond-shape accent tiles contribute fiery colors, just right for a wall behind a gas cooktop.

DESIGNING WITH SHAPE, SIZE, AND PATTERN

Most ceramic tiles are square, but you'll find other shapes, including hexagons, rectangles, and octagons. These often look especially attractive when combined with small squares of a contrasting color. You can arrange square tiles of different colors to produce large patterns. Or turn a square tile 45 degrees and you have a diamond. To frame a pattern, check the many types of narrow border tiles that manufacturers offer.

Small tiles usually make confined spaces look larger; large tiles scale down big rooms. While there are exceptions to every rule, larger tiles usually are a better choice for floors and smaller tiles look more pleasing on walls.

You can define separate areas on a floor by placing tiles at an angle or in swirling patterns. Or create border patterns to set areas apart.

Choose the color and width of your grout lines carefully. Grout that contrasts with the tile will emphasize the geometry of the layout. However, it will also accentuate any imperfections in the installation. If you want to call attention to decorative tiles, choose grout that matches the main background color of the tile.

GROUT WIDTH

Wide grout lines (½ inch usually is the maximum) make sense when you want to emphasize the grid created by the grout or the grout color. Wide grout lines are often necessary when laying irregularly shaped tiles. Thin, dark grout lines add a crisp finish to a project. Light-colored grout creates a neutral base that showcases the color and design of the tile.

This bold entryway features a square-and-cross pattern in the center, which lightly echoes the stained glass pattern on the door. Square accent tiles in two smaller sizes are scattered throughout the floor with subtle symmetry.

Repeating the same border pattern on both wall and floor lends this bathroom a crisp, unified look. Blue dots among white tiles tie the floor to the strong blue color scheme.

Bold tilework can enliven small areas. A hand-painted rooster and randomly placed decorative wall tiles impart charm to this narrow niche.

TILE SIZE

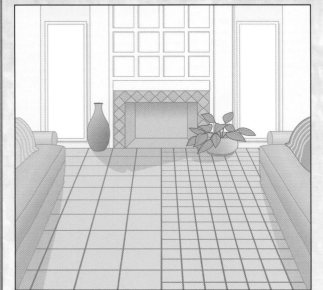

Large tiles call less attention to themselves than smaller tiles and generally look better in larger rooms. Small tiles tend to emphasize the grid of the grout lines and become more of a design element.

Shop tile stores first when exploring the wide range of tiles and related supplies. That's where you'll find hand-painted tiles, tumbled marble, triangular tiles, tiles with stamped impressions, and border tiles of various sizes, textures, and colors. Home centers have a more limited selection, but often at lower prices.

CHOOSING
TILE & GROUT

If you want basic colors at a low price, you can probably pick up all your tile in one trip to a home center. But you will be cheating yourself if you don't also check out at least one store that specializes in tile and stone. Tile stores offer you a connection with manufacturers all over the world. These stores usually stock a dazzling variety of colors and textures and can order even more.

This chapter will help you choose the correct tile for the job to make sure your installation will be beautiful and long-lasting. While searching out the best materials may seem frustrating and time-consuming, the effort you put into considering all tile possibilities will pay off in an installation that expresses your individuality and beautifies your home.

Don't limit yourself to one type of tile. Adding a row or two of tiles in a different color, shape, or texture can enhance the job's appearance at only a little extra cost in materials and work. Pigmented grout offers another choice for design variation.

And, to avoid revealed tile edges—a telltale sign of an amateur job—be sure to buy all the trim tiles you'll need at the same time.

Tile is classified according to how porous it is. Impervious and vitreous tiles absorb very little water and are suitable for places where the tile will become wet or be subjected to freezing temperatures. Semivitreous and nonvitreous tiles are more absorbent.

Nonvitreous	Semivitreous
Vitreous	**Impervious**

FLOOR TILE

You can place floor tile on walls. But never install wall tile on a floor—it will almost certainly crack. Floor tile is usually ⅝ to ⅜ inch thick. Floor tile has to be hard, too, so it can resist wear and water. Because it is so strong, you will probably need a wet saw to make any cut that goes in two directions (see *page 53*).

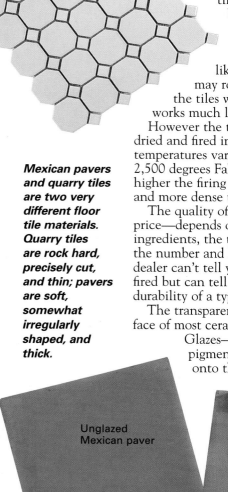

Ceramic floor tile

CERAMIC TILE

Most modern ceramic tile starts as clay, which is combined with other ingredients, such as shale, gypsum, and sand. The mixture of all these elements is called a bisque.

Bisque is then shaped into tiles through one of several methods. Most tile manufacturers extrude tiles by pressing a doughy bisque through a die that's shaped like the tile. Smaller manufacturers may ram a wetter bisque into forms, like pouring concrete, or they may roll the bisque flat and cut out the tiles with a shaped cutter that works much like a cookie cutter.

However the tile is formed, it must then be dried and fired in an oven called a kiln. Kiln temperatures vary from about 900 degrees to 2,500 degrees Fahrenheit. In general, the higher the firing temperature, the stronger and more dense the tile will be.

The quality of a ceramic tile—and its price—depends on the purity of the bisque ingredients, the temperature of the kiln, and the number and length of firings. Your tile dealer can't tell you how a particular tile was fired but can tell you about the strength and durability of a type of tile.

The transparent or colored coating on the face of most ceramic tiles is called a glaze. Glazes—made of lead silicates and pigment—are brushed or sprayed onto the surface of a bisque tile,

Mexican pavers and quarry tiles are two very different floor tile materials. Quarry tiles are rock hard, precisely cut, and thin; pavers are soft, somewhat irregularly shaped, and thick.

which is then fired. The glaze may be applied before or after the bisque has been fired the first time.

Glazes add color to a tile and protect its surface. The hardness of a glaze depends on the temperature of the kiln and the length of time the tile was fired. When purchasing floor tiles, be sure the glaze is hard enough to withstand foot traffic.

Sometimes additives are mixed with glazes to produce textured surfaces. Sawdust is one popular additive; in the kiln the sawdust burns away, leaving the tile surface slightly roughened and, therefore, slip-resistant. Silicone carbide sprinkled on the glaze also roughens the surface.

Porcelain floor tile

QUARRY TILE

Originally, quarry tile came from quarried stone, which was cut, ground, and polished. This process proved very expensive, so tile manufacturers developed an extrusion method for making vitreous clay tile that approaches the hardness of natural stone.

Quarry tiles are hard, unglazed tiles that range in color from light tan to deep red to black. You can install quarry tiles indoors or—in some locations—outdoors. Be sure to apply a sealer; unsealed tiles can stain permanently. Don't install quarry tile on kitchen countertops, however, because the sealer is not suitable for food-preparation surfaces.

Because they are unglazed, quarry tiles provide a somewhat slip-resistant surface. If you want an extremely slip-resistant surface—perhaps for floors elderly persons will use—you can buy quarry tiles with a grid of raised dots.

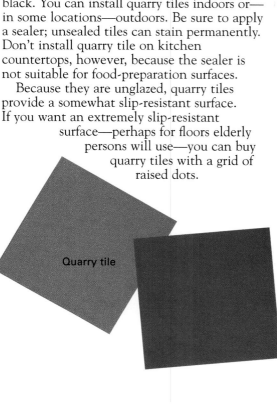

Unglazed Mexican paver

Glazed Mexican paver

Quarry tile

STONE

Tile cut from slabs of natural stone has served as floor covering for many centuries. (See *pages 26 and 27* for more information on various types of stone tile.)

Not all stone tile is durable and strong enough for flooring. Many stone tiles stain easily. And some, such as travertine and various types of marble, are porous, making them difficult to keep clean unless they are well-sealed. Before buying natural stone tile for a floor, ask your dealer for assurances that the particular material has performed acceptably in installations similar to yours.

Stone tiles vary in color and pattern, so tiles from the same batch may be noticeably different. Buy extra; you may need to return some that do not match.

Vermont slate is about ½ inch thick. Its surface is noticeably ridged but is smoother than flagstone. Vermont slate comes in boxes that contain a set number of tiles of various sizes and shapes, designed to fit together in a quiltlike pattern. Cut and install the slate as you would any natural stone (see page 52).

TESTING FOR QUALITY

Floor tile for installation in a dry location, such as a hallway, can be slightly porous. But outdoors, or in other places where the tile will get wet, lay impervious or vitreous tile (see *page 21*). Outdoor tile also must be strong enough not to crack and hard enough to resist stains and scuffs.

Ask your dealer for a tile's rating. The American National Standards Institute (ANSI) divides tile into standard-grade, second-grade, and decorative thin wall tile. ANSI also rates tiles according to porosity, ranking them impervious, vitreous, semivitreous, or nonvitreous.

The PEI Wear Rating System, which applies to many tiles, grades tiles according to their suitabililty for various types of floors.

Here's how to test tile density yourself. Pour a little water on the back of the tile. If the water sits on the tile back for a couple of minutes, the tile is vitreous or impervious and is suitable for all floors. If the water soaks in a little, the tile is semivitreous and good enough for dry floor locations. If the tile soaks up water readily, it is nonvitreous and should not be used on a floor. Or do as the pros do: Touch your tongue to the back of the tile to test it. If your tongue sticks to it a bit, the tile is nonvitreous; if not, the tile is vitreous.

To check hardness, set a sample tile on the floor and try to scuff it up with your hardest heels. If the scuff marks are difficult to clean, consider buying a different tile.

Granite and porcelain tiles are durable enough to serve as floor tiles. Marble scratches more easily, but some varieties are harder than others.

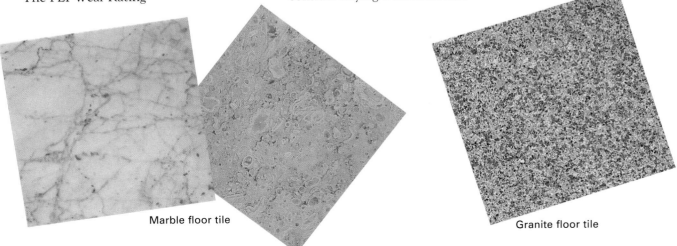

Marble floor tile

Granite floor tile

WALL TILE

Red dot

Border

Brick shape

Octagon

Crackled glaze

Textured border

Unusual wall tiles are not difficult to install, but they may be expensive. It takes only a few stunning tiles to spice up a wall of plain tiles.

Striped

Imprinted for a marble look

Accent tile with imprinted design

Marblelike glaze

Wall tiles aren't as subject to abuse as floor tiles are, so color and style can be your primary selection criteria. **STANDARD WALL TILE:** The most commonly used wall tile is 4¼ inches square. Tabs on the edges near each corner make the tiles self-spacing—just butt them up against each other, and you will automatically have grout lines about ¹⁄₁₆ inch wide. This standard tile is soft, so you can easily drill through it and cut curves or notches with a hand tool (see *page 52*). Its glazed surface is hard enough to withstand scrubbing and bumps, but it would not survive the abuse regularly heaped on floors. Standard wall tile should not be installed outdoors.

Although standard wall tile is often applied to bathtub or shower walls, these tiles are not usually vitreous (see *page 23*), so they absorb water easily. That's why you should not place wall tiles on any horizontal surface where water may sit, such as a ledge around a bathtub. On wet-area wall surfaces, be sure to grout all joints well. When applying new grout, mix the grout powder with latex additive rather than water, for extra strength. After a week or so, apply grout sealer (see *page 31*). Maintain the grout joints to prevent voids; immediately fill in any holes or cracks with grout.

DECORATING OPTIONS: You can easily jazz up a tiled wall by introducing two or more colors in a pattern. Instead of alternating the colors in a checkerboard motif, many decorators prefer to incorporate two or three rows of brightly colored tiles into a field of white or neutral-colored tile.

When mixing two kinds of tile this way, make sure they have the same thickness and the *exact* same width and length. Tiles from different manufacturers may vary in size by ¹⁄₃₂ inch. This may not sound like much, but it is enough to make your grout lines look glaringly misaligned.

Don't be afraid to use nonstandard tiles on walls. Large square or rectangular tiles can look elegant.

Remember that all exposed tile edges should be hidden. Making an edge with regular field tiles looks unprofessional. Install bullnose tiles for edges. You may need trim tiles to make outside corners, too. (see *page 29*).

MOSAIC TILE

1¼" squares

Tiles that measure 3 inches square or smaller are usually called mosaic tiles. Mosaics are normally made of high-quality clay and glaze, and are fired for a long time, making them vitreous. This means the little tiles work well for almost any installation—walls or floors, wet or dry locations, indoors or outdoors.

A grid of small tiles makes a distinctive impression, ideal for a new installation in an older home or to achieve a retro look in a new home. The numerous grout lines make a mosaic floor very slip-resistant.

Mosaics used to be laid one tiny tile at a time—a painstaking task. Today, the small tiles come assembled on sheets, so they are nearly as easy to install as standard tile. A plastic or paper sheet glued to the back of the tiles usually holds back-mounted mosaic tile together. Plastic strips sometimes bind them into a sheet. However they are joined, you just lay the tile sheet in the thin-set adhesive, backing and all. The backing will not interfere with the adhesion.

Grout joints are already established for the tiles on the sheet. However, you must take care to space the sheets so the grout joints between the sheets match the ones between the tiles.

Less common are face-mounted mosaics, joined by a sheet of paper on the face of the tile. To install this kind, leave the paper on during setting, then dampen and remove it after the adhesive has dried.

Mosaic sheets usually come in 1- to 3-foot squares or rectangles. They may be all the same color or set in a pattern of various colors. Some sheets are simple rectangles. Others have interesting shapes or combinations of shapes that fit together perfectly, so you can't see where one sheet ends and another begins.

You can easily make your own mosaic pattern. When you buy the sheets of your predominant tile color, buy some sheets of different-colored tiles of the same size. Cut tiles out of the sheets, install the sheets, then set the colored tiles into the spaces.

Blue dots and white field tiles

Classic 1" octagons

Variegated colors

Mosaics—held together by paper, mesh, or plastic backing—make it easy to cover a wall or floor with thousands of tiny tiles. More difficult is grouting; it takes patience to make sure there aren't voids in the many grout lines.

NATURAL STONE AND PORCELAIN

A combination of color, pattern, and texture gives tiles cut from natural stone a rich look rarely achieved by manufactured products. Your local tile store probably carries stone tiles quarried from near and far. Porcelain tiles look like stone but are more durable.

INSPECTING AND INSTALLING: Most natural stone tiles are sold as pieces 12 inches square and ⅜ inch thick.

Though not always uniform in color or texture, these tiles are just as uniform in size as ceramic tiles. They must be cut with a diamond or masonry blade on a power saw (see *pages 52–53*).

Natural stone isn't rated for strength and density like manufactured ceramic tiles. When you buy stone tiles, examine them for color variations, and don't be surprised if you have to return some for exchange due to damage or discoloration.

Lighter-colored stone tiles are somewhat translucent, so install them with white thin-set. Gray thin-set will cause the tiles to look muddy.

The grout color usually should match the color of the stone tiles. And make the grout lines thin—⅛ inch or less—so you won't detract from the natural beauty of the stone. That way, the entire installation will take on the appearance of a single slab instead of separate tiles.

MARBLE: For thousands of years, marble has been the hallmark of sumptuous interiors and exteriors. Marble is limestone that has been subjected to pressure deep beneath the earth's surface, resulting in a hard structure of crystals with pronounced veins. Marble colors range from almost pure white to nearly black. When other minerals are present, marble takes on colors such as pink, gray, and green.

Some forms of marble are hard and vitreous, while others are soft and absorbent. Some marble can be easily scratched and stained. Marble is usually an excellent choice for walls, but it should be installed for floors only where it will receive little wear. It isn't a good choice for countertops because even the hard varieties can collect stains that are impossible to clean away.

Dark-colored marble may fade noticeably when installed in a sunny location. Marble cracks easily, so it must be installed carefully in mortar that supports it solidly at all points.

The surface of marble may be polished to a high sheen, which will wear away under foot traffic. Other common surface treatments for marble are honed, a smooth matte finish, and tumbled, a pitted and porous surface.

GRANITE: This stone is actually a part of the earth's crust—igneous rock composed of feldspar, quartz, mica, and other minerals. Granite is found all over the world; each deposit has distinctive characteristics and color, ranging from almost pure black to light-colored speckles. Stronger and harder than marble, granite is

Granite

Marble

Marble

Marble

Tumbled marble

Tumbled marble

Tumbled marble

Tumbled marble

Slate

Tumbled marble

Granite tends to be speckled or mottled. Marble has grain lines or splotches of variegated colors. Inspect each piece to make sure all your tiles are similar in appearance.

Tumbled marble has a slightly rough, pitted appearance. Apply sealer to it to make it easy to clean. Slate can be green, gray, blue, or a combination of colors.

MARBLE OR PORCELAIN?

You be the judge: Can you tell the difference between the porcelain and the marble? (Porcelain is shown on the left, marble on the right.)

TRAVERTINE: Quarried in France and only a few other places, travertine consists of layers of calcium carbonate formed by underground deposits near springs. Its color is a mellow brown, and it features interesting veins and a pitted surface. Travertine is rare, so it can be expensive.

AGGLOMERATED STONE: These tiles are manufactured by binding stone particles and dust together with an epoxy resin. The mixture is molded, allowed to harden, then polished to a high gloss. The result is not as attractive or as strong as granite or marble, but it is inexpensive.

PORCELAIN TILE: This new product—a form of ceramic tile—serves as a substitute for a number of materials. Some porcelain tiles look like marble—either highly polished or tumbled—in a wide variety of colors.

Porcelain is more durable and stain-resistant than marble. With simple cleaning, it will retain its appearance through years of heavy use. Some porcelain tiles have a glazed surface with a marblelike design, while others have a single color penetrating all the way through the tile.

Many people cannot tell the difference between porcelain tile and marble; others consider porcelain just an imitation of natural stone. Although porcelain tile does sometimes serve as a substitute for natural marble, it is just as natural as any ceramic tile, made of clay that is fired at very high temperatures.

exceptionally durable. Granite's density—the same as that of vitreous tile—enables it to withstand freezing weather conditions. Granite tile resists staining and remains easy to clean through heavy use.

These qualities make it a particularly versatile tiling material—well suited to the full range of interior or exterior applications, including floors, walls, and even countertops (see *page 82*).

Durable, maintenance-free porcelain is manufactured to resemble many natural materials.

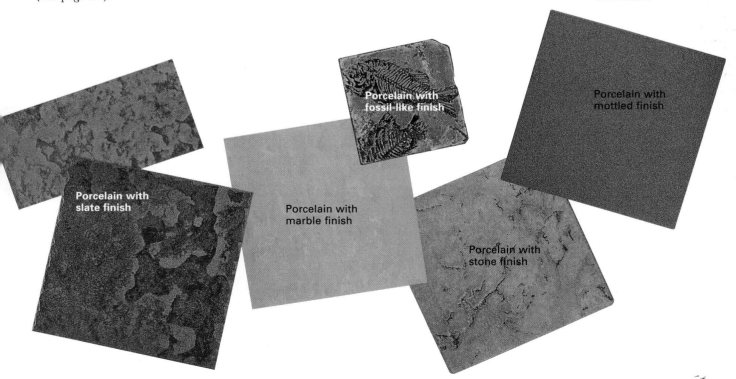

Porcelain with fossil-like finish

Porcelain with mottled finish

Porcelain with slate finish

Porcelain with marble finish

Porcelain with stone finish

CEMENT-BODY TILES, PAVERS, AND BRICK VENEER

If you live where winter doesn't bring wet and freezing weather, you can install almost any floor tile for a patio surface. In most locations, however, freeze/thaw cycles will crack tile, unless it is impervious or vitreous. Slate, granite, porcelain, and many quarry tiles and mosaics work well for outdoor surfaces in cooler climates. Three other types of tile—cement-body tiles, pavers, and brick veneer—are often made specifically for outdoor use. Make sure the tiles you buy are suited for outdoor use; you can ask your tile dealer for assurances that the tile you choose has performed well outdoors in your area. You can also give an interior floor rustic appeal with these tiles.

CEMENT-BODY TILE: These tiles—molded of sand-mix concrete—come in a variety of shapes and colors. They are strong, durable, and inexpensive; but some people find their appearance less appealing than the natural products like stone. You can cut cement-body tile with a wet tile saw or a circular saw equipped with a masonry blade.

PAVERS: Made of fired clay or porcelain, pavers are usually vitreous or semivitreous and may be glazed or unglazed. They range in thickness from ½ inch to 2 inches and can be as large as 2 feet square.

Many handmade pavers from Mexico, Italy, and Portugal are semivitreous so are not suited for outdoor use in areas with colder winters. They are also irregularly shaped, making them a bit difficult to install.

Be sure to seal unglazed pavers that will be set outdoors, using a sealer made for tiles.

BRICK VENEER: These tiles are meant to look like brick without having the weight or thickness of standard bricks. Some are actually thin bricks; others are made from tile bisque ingredients and fired at a low temperature. Some cement-body tiles (see *above*) are shaped and colored to look like brick, too.

Brick veneer tiles are usually about ½ inch thick. All are porous, making them unsuitable for most indoor floors. Check that the brick veneer you choose is vitreous before installing it on an outdoor surface. Grout brick veneer with a grout bag (see *page 71*); if you use a float and sponge, it will be difficult to clean the grout out of the porous veneer.

Cement-body fireplace surround

Cement-body semismooth hexagon

Cement-body semirough 12" 'marble"

Cement-body rough finish

Cement-body smooth terra-cotta tile

Brick-faced tile

Cement-body pavers and natural flagstones make great outdoor patio surfaces or informal interior floors.

Flagstone pavers

TRIM TILE

Most of the tiles in a typical installation—the field tiles—are flat and glazed on one face only. And the unglazed edges aren't meant to be visible when the job is done. Hiding those edges to give a job that finished look is a job for trim tiles: tiles that are glazed and shaped on one or more edges.

Flooring jobs usually don't call for trim tiles because base moldings and thresholds cover the tile edges. Most wall and countertop installations, however, require trim. Here are some common trim tiles.

■ *Bullnose* tile, also called *cap*, has one rounded edge. It provides a finished edge for field tiles. It can serve as countertop edging, too.

■ A *corner* or *down angle* tile has two adjacent bullnose edges to make a corner.

■ *Cove base* tiles fit at the junction between a wall and a floor or countertop to form a continuous tile surface.

■ An *out angle* goes around an outside corner in such an installation.

■ *Radius bullnose* looks like a bullnose, but with a deeper curve. It can edge a countertop.

■ *Radius bullnose down angle* and *up angle* are outside and inside corner tiles to go with radius bullnose.

■ *V-caps* and *V-cap corners* offer another choice for countertop edging. (See *pages 78–81* for more information on countertop trims.)

Buy trim tiles from the manufacturer of the field tiles, when possible. Rarely do two tile makers offer tiles that match exactly in color or size.

If you cannot find the trim tiles you need to finish the edges of your installation, consider other trim options. Wood trim and metal or PVC moldings may do the job. If the field tile is soft, you may be able to round off the edge with a masonry stone, belt sander, or small hand grinder.

Be sure to include the price of trim tiles when calculating the cost of materials. Often, the field tiles are inexpensive but the trim tiles are surprisingly costly.

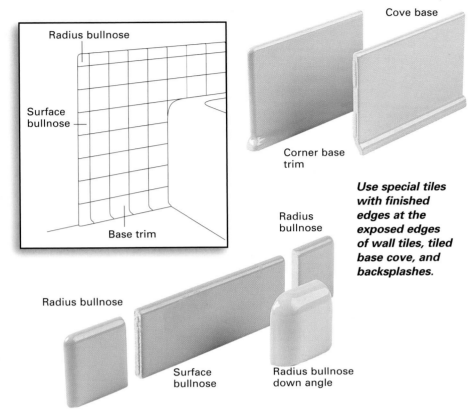

Use special tiles with finished edges at the exposed edges of wall tiles, tiled base cove, and backsplashes.

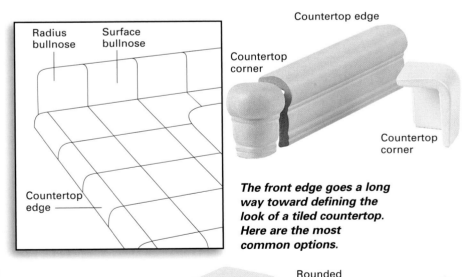

The front edge goes a long way toward defining the look of a tiled countertop. Here are the most common options.

BORDERS AND ACCENT DESIGNS

Ceramic designs

Tiles with different colors, unusual shapes, or intriguing designs can enliven a wall or floor. They are sometimes expensive, but often you need only a few.

BORDERS: Border tiles frame and define a portion of a wall or floor. Lay these narrow tiles in a row for a line of color. A border near the edge of a tile field defines it, or you can divide a tiled area into sections. Border tiles often have a distinctive texture as well as color. Because they are distinctive, borders do not have to be the same length or thickness as the field tiles.

ACCENT TILES: These tiles contrast with the main field of tiles on a floor or wall. They often take the form of dots, tiles much smaller than the field tiles, placed either randomly or in a repeating pattern.

HAND-PAINTED TILES: These tiles are created by craftspeople, who paint the surface of a tile, then fire it. The painted decoration becomes embedded in the glaze, so it cannot be easily scratched. Many painted tiles are fired at low temperatures, so they may not be strong enough for service on floors or countertops. Take advantage of them to accent walls, backsplashes, or fireplace surrounds. You can lay them in the low-traffic corners of floors.

You can find hand-painted tiles in tile stores and at craft fairs and art shows. Many tile artists show samples that you can choose from, or will custom-paint tiles for you. Give the artist a sample of the tile you will be using on the rest of your layout to match for size and thickness.

A group of hand-painted tiles that fit together to create a single picture provides a striking effect. (See an example on *page 19*.)

ANTIQUE TILES: You can often find old tiles at flea markets, antiques stores, and some tile outlets. They can bring authentic old-time charm to an installation. Buy the antiques first, then shop for standard tiles to provide a background color for them. Chances are you will not find tiles of the same size; you may have to trim some standard tiles, or allow an extra-wide grout line around the antique tile. Another option: Frame an antique tile in wood to hang on a wall or use as a trivet.

Relief ceramic

You can let your imagination— and your budget—run wild when choosing accent tiles. Often, only a few expensive tiles are needed.

Stenciled porcelain

Stone mosaic

Ceramic relief

Carved marble

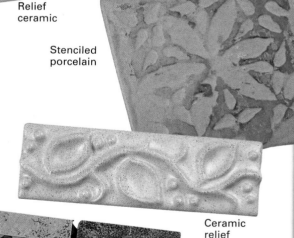

DESIGN YOUR OWN TILE

You can design and paint your own custom tiles at many specialty ceramic stores. Start with tiles that have been bisque-fired but not glazed. You may need to order tiles of the right size. The store will provide a variety of glazes so you can brush on a freehand design or stencil a motif on your tile. Once you've decorated your tile, the store will fire it once or twice. Look in the phone book for specialty ceramic stores.

GROUP AND CAULK

Tiles are the main feature of a tiled surface, but grout and caulk contribute to the overall look, too. Choose them to complement the tile color as well as to protect the tile installation.

GROUT: Grout fills the joints between tiles to protect the tile edges and keep water away from the tile adhesive. Besides meeting these practical needs, grout adds color, which can enhance the beauty of a tile surface.

You can probably find the exact color you want from the wide range of grout colors available. Some tile stores can even custom-tint grout to meet your needs. Don't judge grout color by the dry powder; instead, examine cured samples of the grout, which your tile dealer will have in small sticks that simulate a joint. Place a grout stick between two of your tiles to see what the finished job will look like.

Most grouts have a portland cement base. For best results, buy dry grout powder and mix it with latex or acrylic additive. Ready-mixed grout is convenient, but not as strong and reliable. Though the instructions on the grout package refer to mixing with water, always use a latex or acrylic additive. Grout mixed with the additive is stronger and more flexible, retains its color better, and resists mildew and stains. Grout mixed only with water becomes brittle and is prone to cracking and flaking.

Plain grout works well for joints $\frac{1}{16}$ inch or less—self-spaced wall tiles, in most cases. Sanded grout is best for wider joints—nearly all floor and countertop jobs.

Colored caulk

Apply caulk with a caulking gun. For small jobs, a squeeze tube may do the trick.

SEALING GROUT: Grout is not waterproof. If water sits on it, or if it is subjected to a prolonged spray (as when several people take showers, one after the other), moisture can seep through it and damage the tile adhesive. A grout sealer will improve the grout's ability to shed water. Wait a week or two after grouting before applying the sealer. Reapply sealer once a year, or more often if the area frequently gets wet.

CAULK: Caulk is flexible, grout is not. Apply caulk around sinks and other plumbing fixtures, at inside corners, where the wall or floor tile meets the bathtub, and to fill expansion joints. (An expansion joint is the space between two materials that will not expand and contract at the same rate; see *page 48.*) Soft, puttylike caulk comes in tubes that fit a caulking gun (shown *above*) or in squeeze tubes, like toothpaste tubes.

For surfaces that will be wiped, silicone caulk or tub-and-tile caulk are best. Latex or latex-and-silicone caulk turns muddy-colored and dull if washed often. Tile stores carry caulk in a wide variety of colors, so you can exactly or nearly match the color of your grout.

Pigmented grout

Tile dealers sell grout in many colors, so you can choose one that matches or complements a color present in your tiles.

TILING
PREPARATION

Until recently, most professional tile setters laid floor tile in a 1-inch-thick bed of mortar. Some still do. A mortar-bed installation offers durability and excellent water-resistance, but takes a good deal of time to learn. For do-it-yourselfers (and many pros, for that matter), today's preferred method is to lay down a sheet of cement backerboard, trowel on thin-set adhesive, and set the tiles. The result is just as strong and durable as a mortar-bed installation. And the job requires no special skills, only elbow grease and attention to detail.

Tile adds weight—but not significant strength—to a floor. Tiles laid on a floor that is not sufficiently firm will almost certainly crack. This chapter describes how to strengthen a floor so it can support tile without flexing.

Walls usually require less preparation than floors for tiling. The wall must be smooth and free of large waves. And you should always check walls for plumb; if adjoining walls are out of plumb, you may need to adjust your tile layout to avoid an obviously tapered column of tiles in the corner.

Tile adhesive must stick securely to the wall or floor surface. Slick surfaces must be roughed up before applying adhesive.

Whenever possible, you should move obstructions and not try to tile around them. Toilets, sinks, towel racks, and moldings should all be removed and taken out of the room before you start the tiling job.

Backerboard is usually placed over diagonal plank subflooring in an older bathroom to provide a strong and water-resistant subsurface for new tile. Removing and later reinstalling the toilet and sink, instead of tiling around them, will simplify the project and yield neater results.

FLOOR STRUCTURES

Carpeting and vinyl flooring do not require rigid support, but tile does. A floor that flexes can crack tiles. So even if your home is structurally sound, your wood floors may not be rigid enough to serve as the substrate for a ceramic tile floor.

If your floor has two layers of 1-by lumber or plywood totaling at least 1⅛ inches in thickness and it rests on strong joists spaced no more than 16 inches apart, it is probably strong enough to tile over. Here's a quick test: Jump up and down on the floor at several spots. If you feel a bounce, then either the joists or the subfloor should be strengthened.

FIRMING UP THE SUBFLOOR

Usually, the best way to strengthen a floor is to work from above. You can increase the rigidity of the existing subfloor by adding a layer of backerboard (see *page 45*) or plywood.

PATCHING A FLOOR: The first step in reinforcing your floor is to patch any rotted or damaged areas. Cut out the damaged area, opening it up to a rectangle that spans from joist to joist. You can do this with a circular saw and a handsaw or reciprocating saw. Cut 2×4 or 2×6 blocking pieces to fit tightly between the joists (see *below*), positioning them so they support both the existing floor and the ends of the patch. Attach 2×4 cleats (nailers) to the inside faces of the joists to support the edges of the patch. Install the patch with 2-inch screws, bringing the surface level with the rest of the floor.

ADDING A SUBFLOOR LAYER: The best way to strengthen a floor is to add a layer of backerboard (the best choice) or plywood. Adding a new layer also provides a smooth surface for the adhesive to stick to. Make sure, however, that adding a layer will not raise the finished tile floor more than ¾ inch higher than an adjacent floor; a step that high from one floor to the next might prove awkward. Before adding the overlay, remove all obstacles and scrape away anything on the existing floor that protrudes more than ⅛ inch. Cover the surface with sheets of

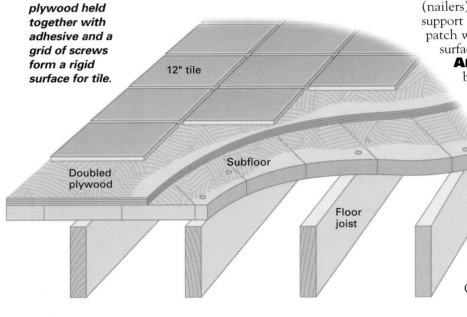

Two sheets of plywood held together with adhesive and a grid of screws form a rigid surface for tile.

12" tile

Doubled plywood

Subfloor

Floor joist

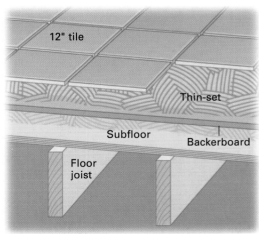

12" tile

Thin-set

Subfloor   Backerboard

Floor joist

Backerboard adds both strength and water resistance, making it an ideal choice for situations where the floor will often get wet.

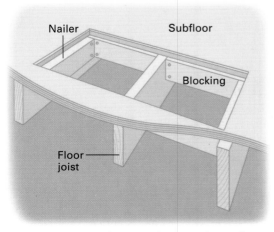

Nailer   Subfloor

Blocking

Floor joist

When patching a floor, make sure the entire perimeter of the patch, as well as the existing surface, is firmly supported.

cement backerboard, roughest side up (see *pages 43–49*), or exterior-grade BC (one good side) plywood, smooth side up.

Start with full sheets, when possible, and arrange the sheets so the joints do not line up with subfloor joints. Cut plywood with a circular saw. See *page 44* for instructions on cutting backerboard.

Fasten the overlay down with screws driven in a grid pattern, 4 to 6 inches apart. Be sure to drive some of the screws into joists.

STRENGTHENING JOISTS

Joists must be free of cracks and the correct size for their span—the distance between supports (see the chart, *right*). If you are tiling a first-floor room over an unfinished ceiling, you'll be able to check and strengthen your joists easily. Otherwise, you will have to remove the ceiling below, or portions of it—a job that may make you think twice about tiling.

If your joists have sagged slightly, you can raise the affected area of the subfloor by tapping in shims or attaching a cleat to the joist (see the box *below*). You can strengthen a joist by installing a new one alongside it. Support the new joist at both ends (you may be able to rest it on the same support as the original joist), and attach it to the old joist with 2½-inch screws, driven every 4 to 6 inches in an alternating pattern.

To add a bit more strength and rigidity, install cross-bridging (see the box *below*).

If your floor sags severely, you can raise and strengthen it with jack posts and a beam. You can do this even if the basement ceiling is finished. To construct the beam, screw two or three pieces of 2-by lumber together. Place the beam under the sagging area, and support it from below with adjustable jack posts. Turn the screws on the posts to push the beam against the ceiling or the joists, and raise it about ½ inch. Wait a week or two and turn the screws again to raise the floor another ½ inch or so. Repeat until the floor reaches the desired level.

JOIST SPANS

In some homes, the joists may be too small for the distance they must span. Local building codes vary, but here is a general guide to tell you whether your joists are large enough. The spans shown are for joists that are spaced 16 inches apart.

Size of Joist	Maximum Span
2×6	9'
2×8	12'
2×10	15'
2×12	18'

STRENGTHENING FLOOR JOISTS

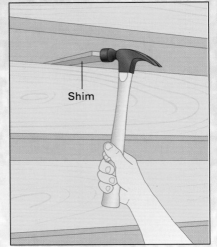

If a joist is strong but has sagged slightly over time, drive in shims to raise the subfloor.

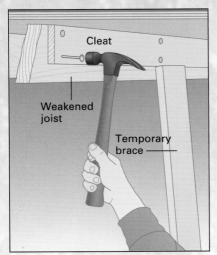

A cleat nailed or screwed to a joist provides extra support for the subfloor and strengthens the joist.

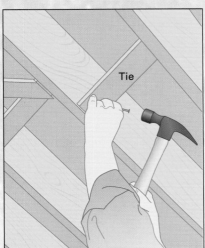

Wood or metal cross-bridging ties the joists together, strengthening the entire structure.

FLOOR STRUCTURES
continued

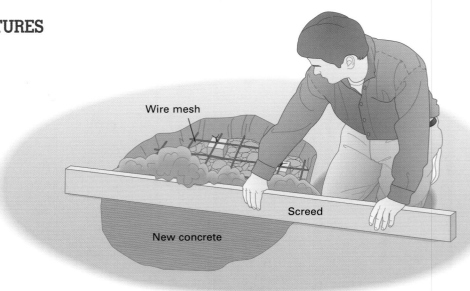

Wire mesh

New concrete

Screed

For a large hole, roughly level the patch with a 2×4 screed, then trowel the surface. Wire mesh will strengthen the new concrete.

PREPARING A CONCRETE FLOOR

A solid, flat concrete slab provides an excellent surface for tile. You should make sure the concrete is stable and that the adhesive will stick to it.

TAKE DOWN HIGH SPOTS: You can fill a few tiny holes or shallow dips (¼ inch or so) when you apply the thin-set mortar, but all high spots must be leveled. Scrape a straight board across the floor to find any bulges in the surface. Then, sand them down with a belt sander and a 40- or 60-grit belt, or pare them down (see *below left*) with a small sledge and masonry chisel.

MAKE SURE IT'S SOUND: Inspect the surface for loose or wobbly sections. If you find one or two small ones, remove them and fill in the hole. Many unstable spots or large ones call for replacing the whole slab. If roots from a nearby tree crack and buckle an

exterior concrete slab, you should consider replacing the slab and removing the tree.

REPAIR HOLES: Patch small holes with patching concrete or sand-mix concrete with portland cement added. Paint the hole with latex concrete bonding agent, fill it, and trowel the surface smooth (see *below right*). To level a large hole, spread the patch material with a 2×4 screed (see *above*).

ISOLATE CRACKS: Cracks will grow over time. To make sure this will not damage your tile or grout, apply an isolation membrane over the cracks (see *page 46*).

ENSURE A GOOD BOND: Thin-set won't bond well to concrete that was treated with an accelerating agent when it was poured. An oily surface also prevents a good bond. Test your concrete surface by sprinkling water on it. If the water doesn't soak in after a few seconds, you should apply a latex bonding agent before troweling on the thin-set.

Remove any high spots on a concrete floor with a small sledge and a masonry chisel.

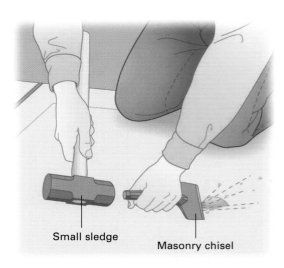

Small sledge

Masonry chisel

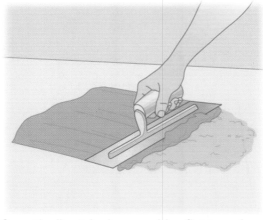

Smooth all patched areas with a flat trowel. Use long, sweeping strokes for larger areas.

FLATTENING FLOOR SURFACES

You may need to level or rough up the surface of a structurally sound floor so the adhesive will stick. This page and the next examine some problems that different types of floors may develop.

Whether tiling a floor or a wall, remove all fixtures and furniture from the room. Cover anything nearby that might be damaged during the tiling work; tape down drop cloths for maximum protection.

Make a realistic estimate of how long the job will take. In addition to the time required to prepare the surface, lay out the job, install tile, grout, and take care of finishing touches, allow at least 24 hours each for the adhesive to cure and grout to set.

DRIVE SCREWS INTO A WOOD FLOOR: If an

area of a wood floor shows a slight hump, or if you hear squeaks or feel the floor flexing in a few places, drive a grid of 2-inch, all-purpose screws into the area (see *left*). A power drill/driver makes the task relatively easy. Most of the screws will only tie the top subflooring layer to the one beneath it. Try to drive some so they penetrate the joist below; you will feel a difference when you hit the joist.

FILL VALLEYS IN A CONCRETE FLOOR:

Concrete floors are often surprisingly wavy. This isn't good for a tile surface, especially if the area will get wet: Standing water can damage grout and the thin-set mortar.

An experienced professional installer can level valleys in a floor by applying a thicker layer of thin-set adhesive over the low spots. For a do-it-yourselfer, the safer method is to straighten the concrete floor before applying the thin-set.

Mason's level

Cordless drill

Utility knife

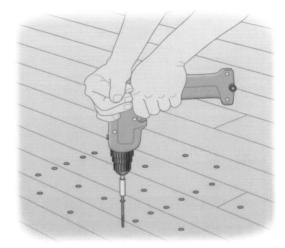

Drive screws through wood flooring into the subfloor to level and strengthen the floor.

Use a straight board and a pencil to draw contour lines indicating valleys in a concrete floor.

Valley

Contour line

FLATTENING FLOOR SURFACES

continued

It takes only a short time to fill in low grout joints with a flat trowel. When they are filled in, troweling the thin-set will be easier.

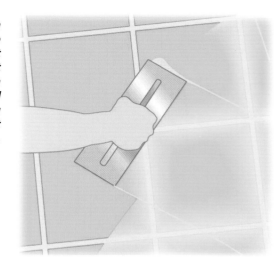

Press gently and take plenty of breaks if you are sanding a large floor; this type of work can harm your lower back.

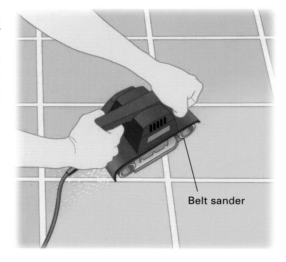

Belt sander

To do this, hold a straightedge so it spans across a valley, and mark the area with a pencil (see *page 37*). Go over the entire floor with the straightedge. Dips of ¼ inch or less are not a problem, but deeper valleys must be filled in. Paint the area with latex concrete bonding agent (the pencil marks will show through when it dries), and apply patching concrete with a flat trowel (see *page 36*). Test the repaired area with the straightedge.

ROUGH UP A PREVIOUSLY TILED FLOOR FOR NEW TILE: You can install new ceramic tile over a sound existing tile floor, but the surface must be rough enough for the new adhesive to stick to. (See *page 42* for information on removing existing tile.)

To prepare an existing tile floor for new tile, first remove any loose tiles. Scrape the old adhesive from the floor and the tile back, and spread thin-set mortar on the back of the tile with a notched trowel. Reinstall the tile, using enough thin-set to match the height of the surrounding tiles.

If the grout in the existing tile has sunken below the tile surface more than ⅛ inch, fill in the joints with grout or thin-set. Scrape the grout diagonally across the joint lines with a large, flat trowel (see *above left*).

Lay an isolation membrane over any cracked tiles or joints (see *pages 46–47*).

New adhesive may not stick to existing tiles with glazed surfaces. Roughen the entire surface with a belt sander equipped with a rough sanding belt—40 or 60 grit. Wear a dust mask and safety glasses. You don't have to press down hard, but you'll have to change sanding belts as they wear out. The sanded surface should feel noticeably rougher than the unsanded surface.

SELF-LEVELING COMPOUND

If your wood or concrete floor is uneven in several places, with dips and low spots no more than 1 inch deep, cover it with self-leveling floor patch. Mix the dry powder with water, then pour the mixture on the floor. Spread it around with a trowel, then let gravity finish the leveling. The surface will dry and be ready for tiling in a few hours. If necessary, set up temporary dams with pieces of lumber to keep the patch material from flowing out of the area you're leveling.

WALL STRUCTURES

Walls to be tiled should be sound, straight, and smooth. Don't count on tile to strengthen an unsound wall or make a wavy one look straight.

HOW WALLS ARE MADE: Older homes have lath-and-plaster walls, in which narrow, rough slats of lath are nailed to the wall studs, running horizontally, with spaces between them. (Sometimes, you'll find metal lath, an expanded metal mesh.) A layer of rough plaster covers the lath, and a thin coat of finish plaster covers that. Drywall (also called wallboard or Sheetrock) covers the walls in most homes built since the 1960s. Sheets of drywall—usually ½ inch thick—are nailed directly to the studs. The joints between the sheets are smoothed with joint compound and tape made of paper or fiberglass mesh. Moisture-resistant greenboard drywall is often installed in damp areas (see *page 43*).

TESTING AND FIRMING A WALL: Push on the wall to be tiled with the heel of your hand; it should feel firm all over. If it doesn't, drive screws or pound nails into studs to firm it up. (An electronic stud sensor will help you find the studs.)

PATCHING: Remove any damaged areas, cutting the hole to a rectangle that spans from stud to stud. Attach cleats to the side of the studs to provide a nailing surface. For drywall construction, patch with drywall of the same thickness. For a plaster wall, attach shims or pieces of lath to the cleats to bring a drywall patch flush with the wall surface around it. Then, apply fiberglass mesh tape to join the patch to either type of wall, and trowel on a coat of joint compound. Allow it to dry, apply one or two more coats of compound, and sand smooth.

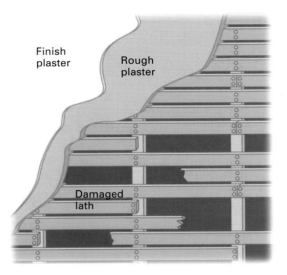

Finish plaster

Rough plaster

Damaged lath

Old plaster sometimes comes loose from the lath. If so, remove it and install a patch using greenboard drywall.

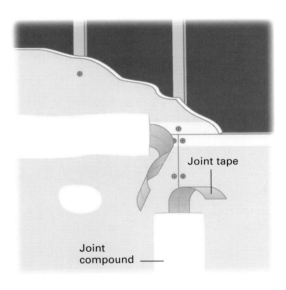

Joint tape

Joint compound

Drywall is simply attached to studs. If a section is broken or weakened due to moisture, remove it and patch with drywall of the same thickness.

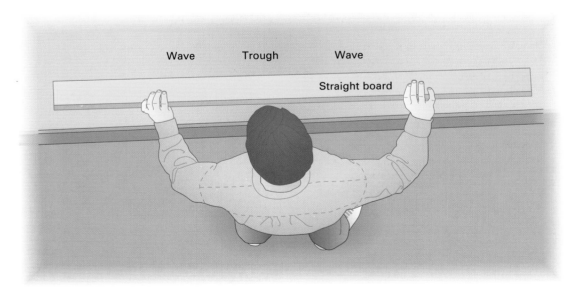

Wave   Trough   Wave

Straight board

Check a wall for waves with a long, straight board. You can fill in waves with joint compound, applied with a large taping trowel. Several coats may be necessary to fill in the trough between the waves. Sand the compound smooth after it has dried.

REMOVING OBSTRUCTIONS

Wherever possible, plan your job so you can cover the edges of tiles with moldings, thresholds, or flanges. Cutting tiles to butt against fixtures or woodwork is difficult and time-consuming, especially if the cuts are not straight. So remove moldings, fixtures, cabinets, and thresholds before tiling, and replace them after the tile is installed.

REMOVING OR CUTTING MOLDINGS

Existing molding that's worn and tired-looking will look even worse next to your new tile floor. Paint it or replace it entirely.

VINYL COVE BASE: This trim scuffs and stains easily, so plan to replace existing vinyl base with new cove base or new wood molding. Pry the cove base away from the wall with a putty knife or flat pry bar. If it is well-stuck, heat the base with a hair dryer or a heat gun (see *below left*) to soften the adhesive.

WOOD MOLDING: Most older base moldings have a base shoe—a thin, rounded piece at the bottom. Remove the shoe in order to install floor tile. On painted moldings, cut the paint along the top of the shoe with a knife, then pry it off with a flat pry bar. Slip a scrap of wood behind the pry bar to prevent marring the base molding. If you work carefully, you may be able to remove the shoe pieces without breaking them. If your base molding has no shoe, remove the whole baseboard. Cut the paint line at its top and pry off the molding with a flat pry bar, protecting the wall with a scrap of wood.

Mark the molding pieces and their locations with matching numbers so you can easily determine where they go when you reinstall them.

CUTTING THE BOTTOM OF CASING: Don't try to cut tiles to fit around a door casing. Instead, cut the bottom of the casing. Place a ceramic tile on the floor next to the casing to act as a guide while you cut the casing bottom with a handsaw (see *below*).

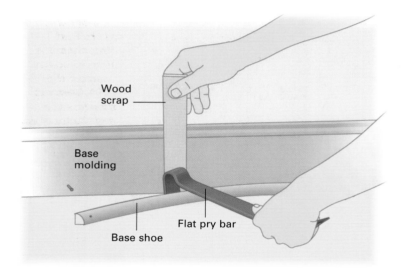

Wood scrap

Base molding

Base shoe

Flat pry bar

Tap a pry bar so its tip slips behind the base shoe. Protect the molding with a scrap of wood, and pry by pulling the bar sideways or up.

Putty knife

Vinyl cove base

Hair dryer or heat gun

A heat gun or hair dryer will soften cove base adhesive, making it easier to remove.

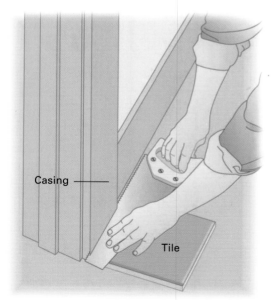

Casing

Tile

Let one of the new floor tiles serve as a guide for cutting casing at the bottom. The thickness of the saw should equal the thickness of the adhesive, making a proper fit when you slide a tile under the casing.

REMOVING PLUMBING FIXTURES

Begin a bathroom tiling job by shutting off the water supply to the toilet and sink. If they do not have stop valves in their supply lines, you will have to shut off water where it enters the house. If you are uncertain about removing a fixture, consult a plumbing book or call a plumber.

SINK: Open the faucet to make sure the water is off. Unscrew the nuts holding the supply lines to the stop valves. Unscrew the nut that connects the drain tailpiece to the P trap (see *below*). Then, lift the sink free of the wall bracket. If it is installed on a vanity cabinet, determine how the cabinet is attached to the wall, and remove it.

TOILET: With the water off, flush the toilet, and sponge all the water you can from the tank and bowl. Disconnect the supply line from the tank. Gently pry off the caps that cover the hold-down bolts for the bowl. Unscrew the nuts on the hold-down bolts; if they are rusted, you may have to cut them.

Most toilets are attached to the floor only, but the tanks of some older toilets are attached to the wall. Detach the tank, if necessary. Then, grab both sides of the bowl and rock it back and forth to loosen it. Lift it straight up to remove from the floor flange (see *below right*). Plug the soil pipe with a rag to keep debris out and sewer gas in. When reinstalling the toilet, you will need a new wax ring and maybe an extender (see box, *above right*).

FLANGE EXTENDER

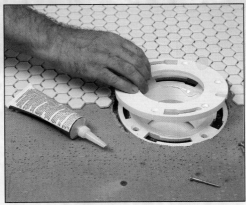

If your new tile surface will stand ½ inch or more above the toilet flange, the toilet may leak when you reinstall it. A flange extender, available from plumbing-supply dealers, will raise it. The type shown attaches with a bead of silicone sealer. Other types use a rubber gasket.

With the water removed, a standard toilet is not too heavy for one person to lift. First disconnect the supply line and unscrew the hold-down nuts, then you can pull the toilet up.

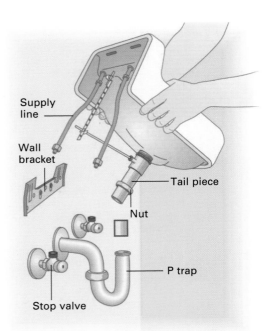

Supply line
Wall bracket
Tail piece
Nut
P trap
Stop valve

Whether your sink is wall-hung (as shown), rests on a pedestal, or sits on a vanity cabinet, disconnect the two supply lines and the P trap to remove it.

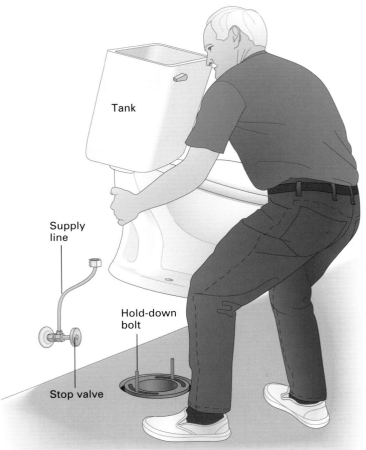

Tank
Supply line
Stop valve
Hold-down bolt

REMOVING EXISTING TILE

Sometimes you can tile over existing tile after filling in grout joints and roughing up the surface (see *page 38*), but old tile usually has to be removed before new tile is installed. Often, this will be a major job.

MORTAR-SET TILE: Before you decide to tear out the old tile, determine how it was installed in the first place. In most older homes and some newer ones, it may be set in a thick bed of mortar. If the caps along the outside edge are radius bullnose instead of standard bullnose (see *page 29*), the tile is probably set in a thick mortar bed. Tile set this way is difficult to remove, and removal may leave a surface too rough for the new installation. Plan to demolish the whole wall or floor, or call in a pro.

PROTECT THE SURROUNDING AREA: Demolition is always a messy business, so protect surrounding surfaces before chipping tiles off a wall or floor. Remove plumbing handles and spouts. Cover a bathtub tightly with red rosin paper or plastic sheeting and masking tape. (If you spread a drop cloth, tile crumbs will work their way under it, and you will scratch the tub when you step on it.) Cram a rag into the drain hole to make sure no dust will clog the drain. Have a bucket ready for hauling away the debris (see *left*).

CHIP AWAY THE TILES: If the tiles were installed with organic mastic, removal should be relatively easy; tiles set in mortar will prove more difficult. First try prying with a putty knife, then turn to a hammer and flat pry bar. You may have to resort to a cold chisel for well-stuck tiles. Hold the prying tool at a steep angle to avoid damaging the underlying wall. Before installing new tile, remove adhesive from the wall and smooth the surface. This can be laborious; a paint scraper may do the trick, or you may have to chip it away with a chisel.

Cold chisel

Handle removed

Spout removed

Red rosin paper

Masking tape

When removing tile, take care not to scratch your bathtub. (Tubs that have been refinished are especially easy to scratch.) Keep all surfaces tightly sealed with rosin paper or plastic, and mend any rips immediately.

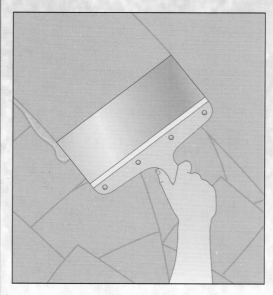

SMOOTHING A SURFACE WITH A SKIM COAT

If the old tiles were set in mortar, you may end up with a very rough surface after chipping away the tiles. Rather than attempting to smooth the surface, you may be better off applying a skim coat to it.

Drag a straight board along the surface to find any high spots, then chip them away with a hammer and chisel. Mix a batch of thin-set mortar, thicker than you would usually make it (see *page 49*). Apply the mortar to the surface with a 6- or 8-inch trowel, then smooth it with a 12-inch trowel. Test the wall for waves and hollows with your straight board from time to time. Don't worry about ridges left by the sides of the trowel; you can scrape them off after the thin-set dries.

If the resulting surface stands out from the surrounding wall, install radius bullnose pieces for the caps and ends (see *page 29*).

INSTALLING SUBSTRATE

You can tile right over an existing wall or floor that is structurally sound, flat, and offers enough tooth for adhesive. Drywall, plaster, and plywood will deteriorate if they become moist, however, so a waterproofing membrane may be required (see *pages 46–47*). If you are installing a new subsurface, use backerboard or greenboard for moisture resistance.

CHOOSING BACKERBOARD

Floor and wall tile used to be installed in a 1- to 2-inch-thick bed of mortar, often reinforced with wire mesh. Some pros still prefer this method, especially for shower floors. However, a simpler approach is to trowel on ¼ inch of thin-set mortar over an appropriate substrate, such as one of these.

CEMENT BACKERBOARD: You'll find many types of backerboard made of cement and cementlike materials. The most common is a ½-inch-thick sandwich of cement between layers of fiberglass mesh. Backerboard often comes in sheets that measure 32 or 36 inches by 60 inches, but you may be able to find larger sizes. Different thicknesses also may be available from tile suppliers.

Another type of cement backerboard incorporates integral fibers (rather than fiberglass mesh) in a mixture of sand and cement. It is typically ¼ inch thick.

Install cement backerboard with special screws; standard drywall screws won't work. Drywall screws are likely to snap when you attempt to drive the heads flush with the surface, and they rust when exposed to moisture. Backerboard screws have ridges under their heads that cut into the surface for a flush fit. They are stronger than standard screws and resist rusting.

GREENBOARD: This drywall, treated to resist moisture, may be either green or blue and comes in ½-inch-thick sheets. It works best on walls that will get wet only once in a while; greenboard cannot stand up to constant or repeated wettings.

Glass-mat gypsum is less common, but can be substituted for greenboard. It takes the form of a sheet of drywall covered with waterproof coating. Although more moisture-resistant than greenboard, it is neither as rotproof nor as strong as cement backerboard. You must seal any cut edges with silicone caulk because only the surface is waterproof.

EXTERIOR PLYWOOD: In low-moisture areas where a substrate is needed to smooth over a wall or subfloor, you can use ½- or ¾-inch exterior (grade BC) plywood.

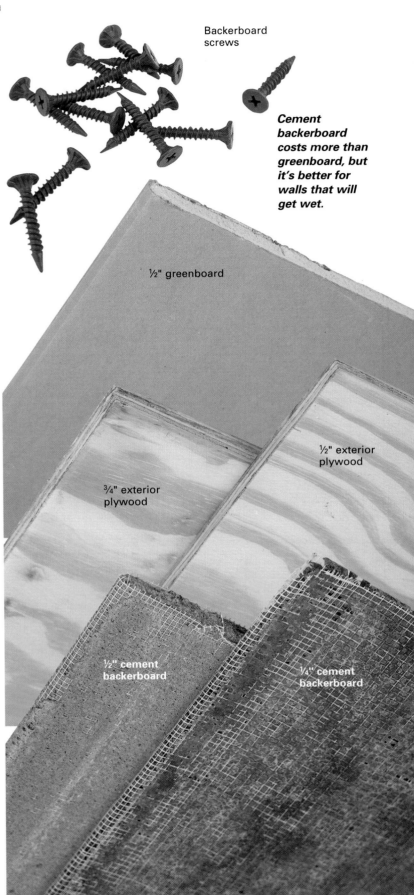

Backerboard screws

Cement backerboard costs more than greenboard, but it's better for walls that will get wet.

½" greenboard

½" exterior plywood

¾" exterior plywood

½" cement backerboard

¼" cement backerboard

INSTALLING SUBSTRATE
continued

CUTTING SUBSTRATE

Cut greenboard or glass-mat gypsum as you would standard drywall: Score a straight line through the paper face into the core, bend the board back along the line to snap the core, then cut the paper on the other side. Cut plywood with a circular saw equipped with a plywood blade. You can drill holes in both materials with standard bits and spade augers.

Cutting cement backerboard calls for a slightly different technique. It cuts best with a backerboard scoring tool,

Backerboard is more difficult to cut than drywall, so hold the straightedge firmly in place as you make several passes with the cutting tool or knife.

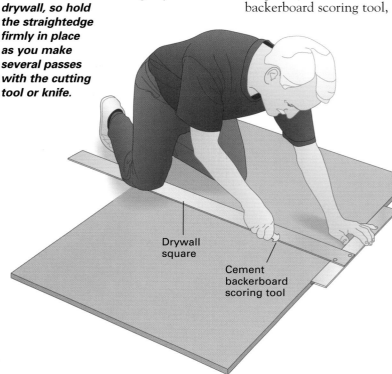

Drywall square

Cement backerboard scoring tool

but you can use your utility knife if you change the blade often. Spread a drop cloth on the floor where you are working, and keep the area clean. Cement backerboard crumbs will quickly scratch floors.

MEASURE: The edges of cement backerboard are rough after cutting, so subtract ¼ inch from each measurement you take. Instead of drawing a cutting line, just mark a point and hold a drywall square against it. You also could mark the top and bottom of the cut, and place a straightedge alongside them.

CUT THE FACE: Hold the drywall square or straightedge firmly in place, and cut by pulling the knife or cutting tool along the straightedge. Make several passes until you have cut completely through the fiberglass mesh. Turn the board over, or grasp it from the other side, and fold it back along the line until it snaps. Cut through the mesh on the other side, and pull the cutoff away. Scrape the cut edge with a tiling stone or the side of a putty knife to smooth it (see *below*).

CUTTING A HOLE: The quickest and neatest way to cut a hole is with a carbide-tipped hole saw in a drill (see *below left*). Mark the center of the hole, then bore through the board with the right size of hole saw. If you need only a few holes, you can cut a circle in front with a utility knife or backerboard cutting tool, making sure you slice through the mesh. Tap the center of the hole with a hammer until it bulges out the back. Cut through the mesh on the back, and remove the center of the hole.

OTHER METHODS: You can cut backerboard using a hand-held wet saw (see *page 82*) or a reciprocating saw. You can even saw it with a dry masonry blade in a circular saw, but this creates a lot of dust (wear a face mask), and it might damage the saw.

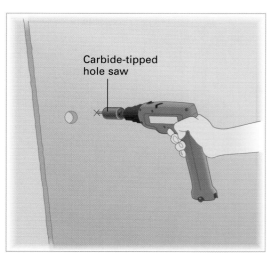

Carbide-tipped hole saw

A drill with a carbide-tipped hole saw makes quick and neat work of hole cutting.

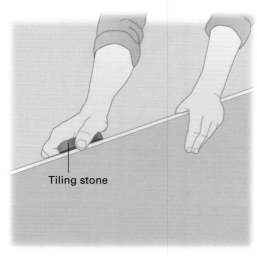

Tiling stone

Smooth the cut edge of cement backerboard with a stone or the edge of a metal tool.

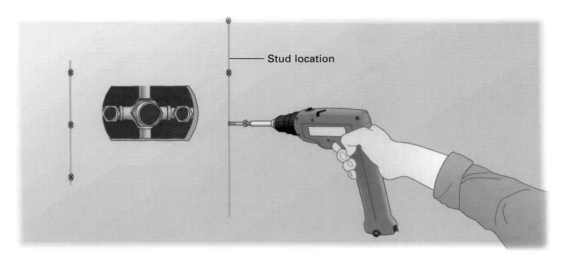

Stud location

Chalk lines marking the locations of studs will make the job faster and neater.

INSTALLING BACKERBOARD

Water doesn't damage cement backerboard, but moisture can seep through it and damage underlying subflooring or walls. Seal a wood subfloor that is likely to get wet with a waterproofing membrane (see *pages 46–47*) before putting down backerboard. Install backerboard with the rougher side out.

ON WALLS: Attach backerboard directly to wall studs, or install it over existing drywall or plaster. Drive backerboard screws so that they penetrate at least an inch into the studs.

ON FLOORS: Cut sheets of backerboard so their seams don't lie directly over the seams in the subflooring below. Measure and mark your baseboard to show the locations of joists so you can see where to drive some of the screws into the joists.

Cut the pieces to allow a ⅛-inch gap between the sheets, and a ¼-inch gap where a sheet meets a wall, bathtub, shower pad, or any other vertical surface. Cut all the pieces first, and lay them on the floor to make sure they fit.

Mix a batch of thin-set mortar according to manufacturer's instructions (see *page 68*). Pick up one or two pieces of backerboard, and sweep the floor beneath clean of crumbs. With a notched trowel, spread an even coating of thin-set on the floor, then press the sheet into it (see *center right*).

Drive in backerboard screws in a grid pattern, with the screws spaced about 6 inches apart. Drive screws into the subflooring and into joists in some places. It's okay to screw the board's ends to the subfloor only.

TAPE THE JOINTS: Lay fiberglass mesh tape (not paper joint tape) over each joint, and spread thin-set over the tape with a flat trowel. Force thin-set into the joints, and feather the edges for a smooth finish.

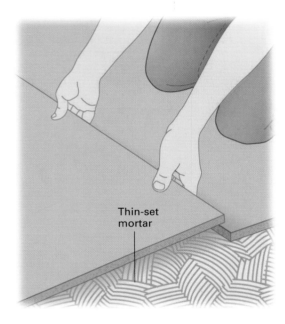

Thin-set mortar

Lay sheets of backerboard for flooring in a bed of thin-set mortar, then drive screws spaced about 6 inches apart.

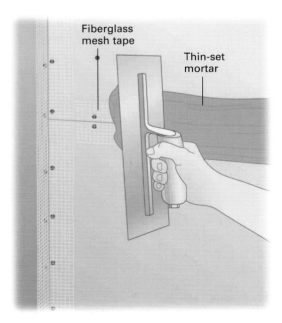

Fiberglass mesh tape

Thin-set mortar

Apply mesh tape to all joints, and spread a smooth layer of thin-set over the tape. Low spots are okay, but make sure the thin-set does not peak much above the backerboard surface.

INSTALLING MEMBRANES

Tiles usually can be set in thin-set mortar or organic mastic directly onto a sound subsurface. But tiles sometime need the extra protection of a membrane beneath them. Membranes can isolate tiles from subsurface conditions, or they can protect the subsurface from water seeping through grout.

ISOLATION MEMBRANES

Cracks in the surface beneath the tiles will probably grow in time, causing the grout, or even the tiles themselves, to crack. And if two types of surfaces underlie a tile surface, they may expand and contract at different rates, damaging the tiles over them. Isolation membranes prevent problems below from spreading upward.

OVER A CRACK: To lay tile over a crack in a concrete surface, apply a two-part membrane of fiberglass mesh and a patching paste (see the photo *at bottom*). Trowel or roll paste over the crack, lay the mesh in it, and trowel or roll on more paste, feathering the edges smooth.

WHERE TWO SUBSURFACES MEET: If two concrete slabs—or a concrete slab and a wood floor—meet under your tiles, lay an isolation membrane (ECB, polyethylene sheet, or tar paper) over the junction so your tiles will rest on a single, stable surface. Apply a coat of thin-set, 2 feet wide or wider, over the joint. Lay the sheet material in the thin-set, and smooth it

Polyethylene

Tar paper (roofing felt)

A variety of products, including liquids, meshes, and sheets, can be used to waterproof a subfloor and protect tile from cracking.

with a roller or straight board. Allow it to set before laying the tiles.

IN A CORNER FOR COVE TILE: A wall is separate from—and moves in different ways than—the floor it rests on. If you will be installing cove tile between wall and floor tile, install a membrane at the junction of the wall and floor as you would over a floor crack.

WATERPROOFING MEMBRANES

Tiles, grout, mortar, and backerboard may not be damaged by water, but water can seep through them and damage the surface beneath. So install a waterproofing membrane wherever you expect a tile floor or wall to get wet.

TAR PAPER: Staple tar paper (also called roofing felt) to wall studs, wood flooring, or drywall before applying backerboard. Increase a floor's ability to shed water by first spreading a layer of roofing cement, then lay the tar paper over it. Roll the paper out carefully to avoid making creases and bubbles. Wait a day or so for the cement to harden before laying the tiles.

POLYETHYLENE: Plastic sheeting is another inexpensive option. Lay it the same way you would tar paper.

TROWEL-APPLIED MEMBRANES: The best of several varieties available contain sand, cement, and latex.

The product may be ready-mixed or you may need to mix the dry and liquid portions together, following the manufacturer's directions. Apply it with a large trowel that has both notched and smooth edges. Spread the material over the floor first with the smooth edge, pushing downward to make a sure bond. Then trowel the material to an even thickness with the notched edge. On the final pass, make long, sweeping strokes with the smooth edge to even it all out. Manufacturers sometimes supply a simple depth gauge to make sure the product is spread in consistent thickness.

You can isolate cracks or joints at the same time you protect the floor from moisture. Embed fiberglass mesh in the membrane material, smooth the mesh, then trowel over it with more membrane to smooth the surface.

Mesh

Waterproofing liquid

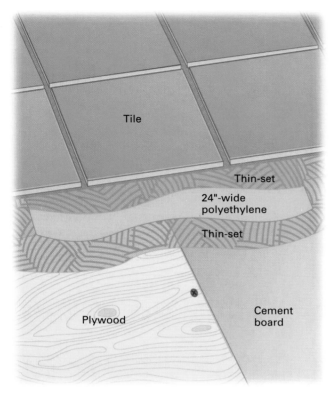

Over cracks or where two different floor materials meet, embed a 2-foot-wide sheet of polyethylene in thin-set to isolate the tiles from the two subsurfaces.

Spread a trowel-applied membrane in three steps: first with the smooth edge of the trowel, next with the notched edge, then with the smooth edge again.

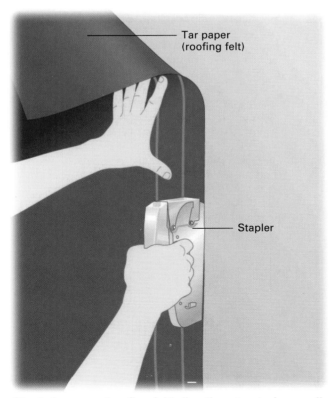

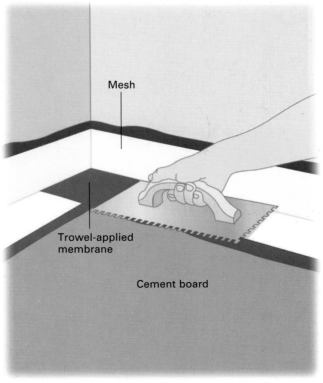

Staple tar paper (roofing felt) directly onto studs, a wall, or floor before installing backerboard.

To prevent cracks when both the floor and wall will be tiled, apply an isolation membrane to the corners.

EXPANSION JOINTS

Seal the hole around a pipe with caulk instead of grout.

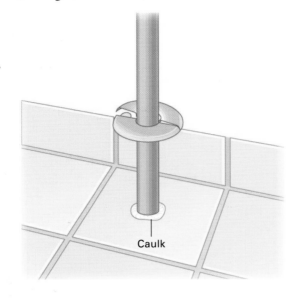

Caulk

When there will be a base molding, install both the backerboard and the tile about ⅛ inch away from the wall. When installing tile as a base molding, caulk the joint instead of grouting it.

⅛" gap

Walls and floors will move independently. Here, a foam strip and a bead of caulk allow that movement without stressing floor tiles or grout.

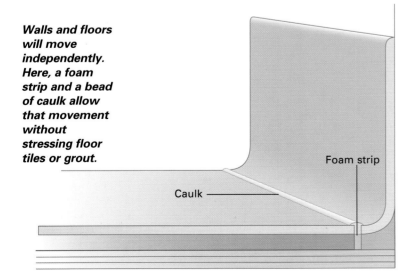

Foam strip

Caulk

When professionals lay tiles on large expanses of floor, they install flexible joints about every 24 feet or so. These joints, which are usually made to look like grout joints, prevent tile and grout from cracking when tiles expand and contract due to changing temperatures. You probably won't lay a floor that large, but you might need expansion joints where tile edges meet a different material or at inside corners.

Installing expansion joints usually is simply a matter of filling the space between tiles with flexible caulk rather than grout. (See *pages 58–59* for caulking techniques.) You can purchase silicone caulk that matches your grout color at most tile stores.

WHERE TILE ABUTS A DIFFERENT SURFACE: Whenever ceramic tile meets woodwork, a plumbing fixture, a pipe, or any other dissimilar surface, you should fill the gap with flexible caulk instead of inflexible grout. Grout could either crack or cause the tile to crack. (If a piece of molding or a threshold will cover the edge of the tile, just leave an empty gap between the tile and the wall or flooring.)

AT INSIDE CORNERS: Wherever two perpendicular tile surfaces meet and no molding covers the gap, caulk the gap instead of grouting it.

Backerboard on floors should be installed with gaps wherever it abuts the wall (see *page 45*). When installing cove tile on the wall to produce a continuous tile surface running from floor to wall, leave a larger gap for the backerboard where the joint between the cove tile and floor tile will be. Place a special foam strip (available from tile dealers) in the space. After setting the tiles, fill the gap with caulk, not grout.

ALONG AN EXPANSE OF FLOOR TILE: If you tile a large floor, place expansion joints every 24 feet for interior floors and every 16 feet for patio surfaces. Apply caulk, not grout in each joint.

If you are not sure that your subsurface is stable, you can install expansion joints every 5 or 6 feet to reduce the possibility of tile damage. However, the best solution is to fix the substructure so that it is firm and stable (see *pages 34–36 and 43–45*).

CHOOSING ADHESIVES

For most residential projects, wall tiles should be set with organic mastic, floors and outdoor tiles in thin-set mortar. However, the type of tile you install and the condition of your substrate may require some other adhesives. Here are your four choices:

ORGANIC MASTIC: This petroleum- or latex-based product comes ready-mixed and is inexpensive. Tiles stick to it immediately, so most wall tiles will not slide downward before it is set.

However, organic mastic does not provide the strength of thin-set mortar, and once dry is not as flexible as thin-set that has been mixed with latex additive. And you cannot level a substrate that isn't perfectly flat with an organic mastic as you can with thin-set. This product works best for tiling over walls that are in good condition. Do a thorough job of grouting, caulking, and sealing the grout; moisture that seeps through can loosen the bond of organic mastic.

Ready-mixed organic floor tile adhesive may be strong enough for small jobs, but it is not as reliable as thin-set mortar.

THIN-SET MORTAR: You mix this powder with liquid shortly before application. Tiles do not stick to it immediately, and once it starts to set, you cannot move the tiles without breaking the bond. But the bond it forms is very strong and resistant (though not impervious) to moisture damage. Thin-set is usually the best product for tiling floors.

Standard thin-set mixed only with water will be firm but easily cracked. Always mix thin-set with latex additive instead of water for greater strength. You can purchase bags of thin-set fortified with powdered latex additive, to which you just add water. This product is nearly as strong as standard thin-set mixed with liquid latex.

BRICK MORTAR: This is the product masons build brick and block walls with. Coarser than thin-set, you can use it for some outdoor projects (see *pages 86–87*).

EPOXY THIN-SET: This comes in three parts: a resin, a hardener, and a powder. It is expensive but offers advantages for special situations. It hardens quickly, perhaps allowing you to set tiles and grout the same day, and water won't damage it. It makes a tight bond with hard-to-glue tiles and substrates, too.

½" drill

Mixing paddle

You can mix thin-set in a bucket by hand, using a stout scraping tool. If you have to mix a number of buckets, rent a heavy-duty ½-inch drill (a standard ⅜-inch drill will probably burn out) and a mixing paddle. Wedge the bucket firmly between your feet to keep it from spinning as you work (see above).

THIN-SET: POWDERED OR READY-MIXED?

You will find ready-mixed thin-set adhesive at a home center, but not at most tiling stores. Some ready-mixes even claim to work as both adhesive and grout. These products will be easier to use than powdered thin-set mortar with liquid latex added to it, but they do not bond as firmly.

The tools shown here will enable you to lay out the job, apply adhesive, measure and cut tiles, grout, and caulk either a wall or a floor.

Wet saw

Snap cutter

Nibbling tool

Mixing paddle

Hacksaw with rod-saw blade

Bucket

Grout float

Stone

Carpenter's pencil

Beater block

Carbide-tipped hole saw

Combination square

Rubber mallet

Sponge

Grout sealer

Squeegee

Square-notched trowel

Straight-edge trowel

Kneelers

½" drill

Caulking gun

Caulk finishing tool

¼" notched trowel

Point-notched trowel

INSTALLING TILE

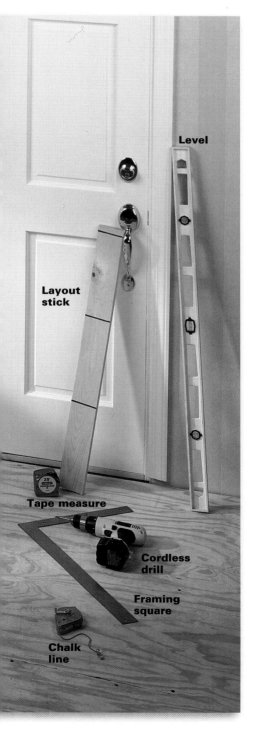

Level

Layout stick

Tape measure

Cordless drill

Framing square

Chalk line

Once you've determined that your floor or wall is sound and is covered with a suitable substrate, you are ready to start tiling. This chapter takes you through the basic steps for simple floor and wall projects. On pages 62, 63, 74, and 75 you will find examples of more- complicated projects, complete with layout and installation tips.

Most tile-setting tools are inexpensive, so don't hesitate to purchase a tool that will make the job go smoothly and produce professional-looking results. You can rent the expensive tools, like a wet saw.

Handy tools for laying out the job include a level, framing square, chalk line, and tape measure. You'll learn how to make a layout stick (called a jury stick) to help with a complicated floor layout (see page 65).

You can mix large amounts of thin-set mortar with a heavy-duty ½-inch drill equipped with a mixing paddle. You'll need several trowels: a square-notched one to spread thin-set on a floor, a point-notched one to apply organic mastic on a wall, and a long, flat one for leveling thin-set on an uneven floor.

You can cut tiles with a wet saw, snap cutter, nibbling tool, or rod saw. Smooth tile edges after cutting with a rubbing stone. A portable power drill with a tile bit or a carbide-tipped hole saw will make holes in tile. (Pages 52 and 53 describe these tools and others in detail.)

A rubber mallet or a beater block will help ensure that the tiles are completely embedded in the adhesive and are level. If you are working on a floor, spare your knees with a pair of kneelers.

Apply and wipe away grout with a laminated grout float, and clean up with a large sponge and a squeegee. Caulk inside corners with a caulking gun.

CUTTING TILE AND STONE

When it's time to cut the tile, the adhesive probably will already be laid or at least mixed, so you will need to work pretty quickly. Practice making accurate cuts in tile before the job begins. If you have only a few difficult cuts to make, a home center or tile dealer will often do them for you for a small fee. However, they may not guarantee that their cuts will be precise.

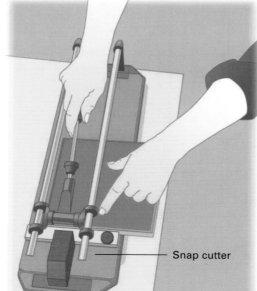

Nibbling tool

One way to notch a tile is to make a series of cuts with a wet saw, then break out the waste with a nibbling tool.

THE RIGHT TOOLS FOR THE MATERIAL

Be sure you have the tools you need for all of your cuts. You may need to make straight cuts, cutouts (cuts that go in two directions), and holes. Before you start laying tile, try out the tools on scrap tiles.

CERAMIC TILES: Any of the tools shown on these pages will cut soft ceramic wall tiles. For most jobs, a snap cutter, rod saw, and drill with masonry bit will be all that you need. You can cut straight edges on most glazed ceramic floor tiles, quarry tiles, and porcelain tiles with a snap cutter. But because floor tiles are thick and hard, making cutouts in them will be more difficult.

If you have only a few cutouts that do not have to be precise, cut them with a nibbling tool. A circular saw equipped with a masonry blade will also do the job. Cut slowly to let the blade grind through the tile.

The best solution is to rent a wet tile-cutting saw. Or, purchase a hand-held wet saw with a diamond blade (see *page 82*).

STONE AND PAVERS: Cuts of any kind—even straight cuts—in marble, granite, slate, and other natural stone tiles require a wet saw. You can rent a tile-cutting wet saw or purchase a hand-held wet saw with a diamond blade. Most pavers also must be cut with a wet saw, although some can be straight-cut with a snap cutter.

MAKING THE CUTS

Make the quality of the cut fit the particular situation. A cut that will be covered by molding does not have to be exact or smooth. If the entire face of the tile will be visible, however, the cut must be precise. Mark tiles for cutting and trimming with a felt-tipped pen, a pencil, or a crayon.

SNAP CUTTER: To cut a tile with this device—which works like a glass cutter—press the tile against the cutter's guide, and align the cutting wheel with your cut mark.

Then score the tile with the cutting wheel. The wheel starts at the front on some machines, the back on others. Push (or pull) the handle while pressing down on the tile. You should hear a scratching noise and see a light cut mark. Score the entire cut in one pass. Press down firmly on the handle to snap the tile. Some cutters include an adjustable fence that slides against the tile and tightens in place to cut a series of tiles to the same size.

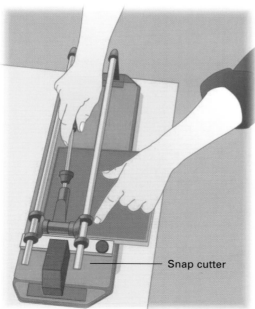

Snap cutter

An inexpensive snap cutter will make straight, one-direction cuts in any tile, but not in stone.

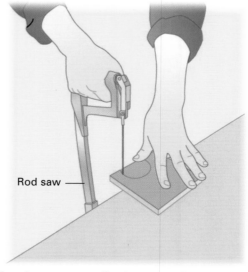

Rod saw

A rod saw cuts easily through soft materials like wall tile. Hold the tile firmly against a flat surface while you work.

USING A SPIRAL SAW

The spiral saw, a relatively new tool on the market, can cut through almost any material, including backerboard, greenboard, marble, and most ceramic tiles. It is not recommended for cutting stone or floor tile. Use it for cuts that will be covered by molding or a flange.

USING A RUBBING STONE

This basic tool will rub away the sharp edge left by a snap cutter. It's handy for rounding off the edges of soft materials like pavers and marble. And if you need to shave just a tiny bit off a wall tile, rub the stone on it with long, even strokes.

NIBBLING TOOL (NIPPERS): This pliers-like tool makes rough cutouts in wall tile. Begin by scoring the outline of the cut with the cutting wheel of a snap cutter. Then carefully nibble away at the tile, removing the waste one "bite" at a time. (Be patient: You may destroy a tile or two before you get the knack of using this tool.)

A nibbling tool allows you to cut a narrow sliver off a tile. Score the cut line and nibble along it.

WET SAW: You usually place the tile against the fence on this tool's sliding table, and push it into the saw blade. Ask for operating instructions at the rental store. You will need to keep one end of a hose in a bucket of water, which you will periodically refill by emptying the saw's tub into it. (Stop cutting immediately if the water runs out.)

ROD SAW: This grit-coated rod attaches to a standard hacksaw. It cuts through soft wall tile easily, but doesn't work very well on heavy floor tile.

Pick up a wet saw from the rental yard only after you are ready to make all the cuts to avoid paying for an extra day.

Carbide-tipped bit

To cut a hole, use a carbide-tipped hole saw (shown on page 44), or drill a series of holes with a masonry bit and punch out the middle.

Wet saw

INSTALLING WALL TILE

Once your walls are covered with a solid substrate (see *pages 43–45*), you're ready to lay out and install wall tile. The next six pages explain the basic steps for most wall tile jobs. *Pages 60 and 61* have special instructions for tiling a tub surround, and *pages 62 and 63* show how to solve some special layout and installation problems.

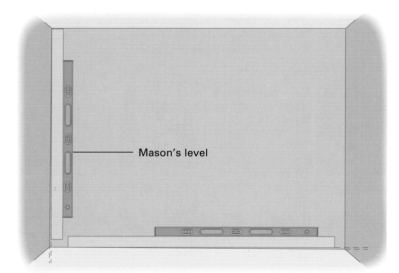

Test horizontal surfaces and walls for level and plumb. If a tiled edge will be noticeably out of square, you need to determine how best to hide the imperfection. The best solution may be to even out a surface.

Mason's level

LAYING OUT THE JOB

Plan the placement of tiles with these considerations in mind:
■ Avoid slivers of tile. This is especially important when an abutting wall is wavy or out of plumb. Differences in tile widths to accommodate a slope or curve will stand out more when tiles are narrow.
■ Arrange the tiles so narrower ones at each end of a wall will be the same size, giving the installation a symmetrical look.

CHECK THE WALLS: Hold a level against the edge of a straight board, and place it against the walls to check for plumb. Also, test all horizontal surfaces—floor, countertop, windowsills—for level. If the walls are plumb and horizontal surfaces are level, then the areas to be tiled will be square to each other. If not, take measurements to see how far out of square they are.

If a wall is more than ¼ inch out of square in 8 feet, the imperfection will be noticeable after the wall is tiled. If an abutting surface is severely out of square or is noticeably wavy, you may want to add moldings or feather out a wall with joint compound to correct the situation. Otherwise, you'll have to trim tiles to fit in that corner so that the imperfection will be less noticeable.

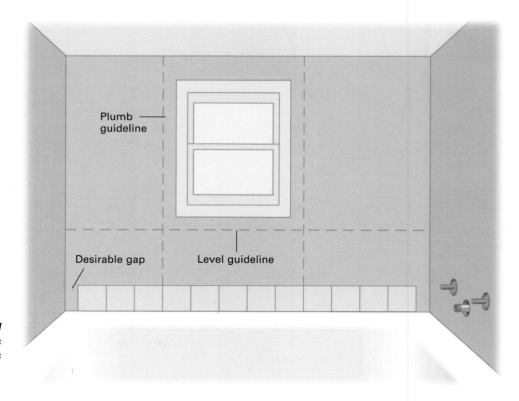

Plumb guideline

Desirable gap

Level guideline

Plan a layout to avoid slivers of tile at the corners and around obstructions such as a window.

DRAW REFERENCE LINES: Mark the center of the wall. Then lean a row of tiles in a dry run from the mark to the abutting wall. If the last tile will be half-width or wider, draw a plumb line from the center mark and designate it your vertical reference line. If the last tile will be a sliver, center the first tile on the center mark and try again. Test with a dry run in both directions from the center. Take into account obstructions, such as doors or windows, so you won't have sliver tiles alongside them.

Also mark a level horizontal reference line as well. If the bottom row of tile will be covered with molding, start the bottom row about ½ inch above the floor or horizontal surface. If it will not be covered with molding and the adjoining surface is straight and horizontal, place a full tile at the bottom. Otherwise, plan to cut the bottom tiles so you'll trim off no more than a quarter of each one.

If a wall will end on an outside corner (see *page 57*), start your layout at the outside corner, where there will be a bullnose tile. If this creates a sliver at the other end of the wall, you can install half of a field tile next to the bullnose edge.

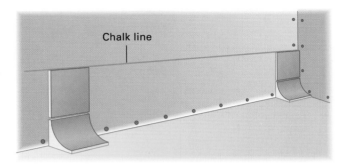

Chalk line

Thin pieces make an out-of-plumb wall obvious.

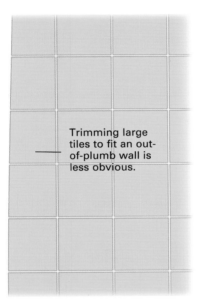

Trimming large tiles to fit an out-of-plumb wall is less obvious.

When laying out for cove tiles, take the thickness of the floor tiles and the floor mortar into account.

If an abutting wall is out of plumb, the imperfection will be more noticeable if the end tiles are narrow. Lay out to allow nearly full-sized tiles at this location.

MAP A TILE DESIGN

A simple and fun way to add color and interest to a wall of tiles is to add a pattern of accent tiles that are the same size as the field tiles. Use a row or two of accent tiles, make a modified checkerboard design, or sprinkle the wall with accents in a random arrangement.

Do a dry run of tiles to determine how many will fit on your wall. Then draw a design on graph paper, letting each square represent one tile. Color the squares to better visualize the finished effect. Include the bullnose caps and corners at the exposed ends of the installation. You may have to draw a number of layouts before you're satisfied.

INSTALLING WALL TILE
continued

When you have decided where every tile will go and have drawn layout lines on the wall, it's time to spread the adhesive. Organic mastic is a good choice for most walls (see *page 49*). For cutting tiles, see *pages 52 and 53*.

ATTACH A BATTEN BOARD: Tiles will stick to organic mastic before the mastic sets, but they may creep down the wall slightly. To ensure that this doesn't happen, attach a straight board as a temporary batten at the horizontal layout line. Rest the first row of tiles on it. Remove the batten later to install the bottom row.

TROWEL ON THE ADHESIVE: Mastic requires a trowel with pointed notches; the mastic container will specify the notch size. Trowel mastic onto a section of wall about 5 feet by 5 feet. Apply it with long strokes for an even surface, and don't leave blobs of mastic on the wall. Don't cover up layout lines or apply mastic beyond the area to be tiled.

SET THE TILE: Install the full tiles in a section, then go back and cut tiles for the corners. Press each tile into place with a very slight twist, inserting spacers as you go, if necessary. Avoid sliding a tile into place—that will squeeze adhesive up into the joints.

Check the surface periodically with a straight board to make sure it's level. Tap the board to set raised tiles a bit deeper into the mastic. If a tile has sunk below the level of its neighbors, pry it out, butter the back with mastic, and press it back into place.

Set the first tiles on a wall in a pyramid shape to make sure you are starting out straight and square. Follow one of the sequences shown.

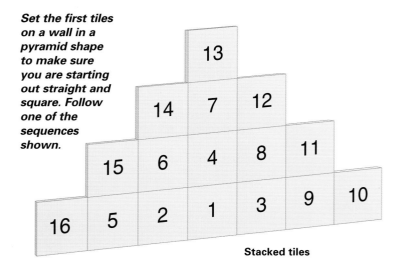

Stacked tiles

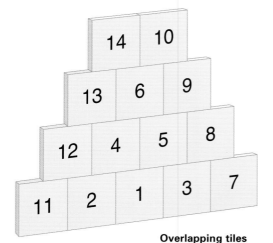

Overlapping tiles

A batten ensures that you start out the job with a straight row. It also prevents tiles from sliding down the wall before the adhesive sets.

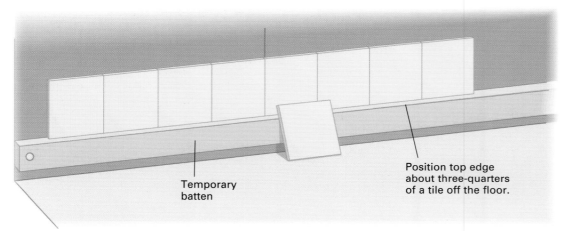

Temporary batten

Position top edge about three-quarters of a tile off the floor.

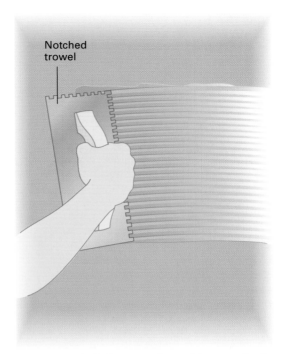

Apply mastic in long strokes with a notched trowel so that it forms a smooth, level surface.

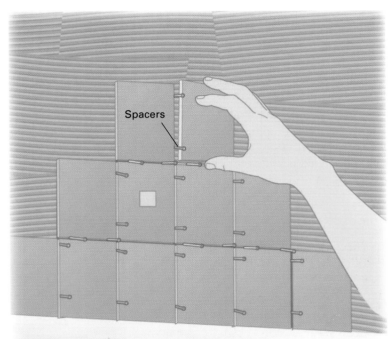

Set each tile into place with a slight twist to make sure the mastic adheres fully. Use nails as spacers between the tiles.

TILING OUTSIDE CORNERS

An outside corner presents unique problems, especially if—as is usually the case—the corner is not plumb in both directions. Try to use whole tiles on the corner, with bullnose tiles overlapping the field tiles. Finding the best approach may take some experimenting. For example, if a wall is only slightly out of plumb and not very wide, you can get away with lining up the bullnose tiles so they will evenly overlap the field tiles. The column of bullnose tiles may be slightly out of plumb but still not noticeable if the corner has whole tiles crisply meeting along the same grout lines. However, if the edge of one wall is badly out of plumb, you may want to install your field tiles there, trimming them as necessary. Then you can overlap the cut edge with whole bullnose tiles.

Install tiles on both walls at the same time so that you can be sure that the bullnose pieces uniformly cover the edges of the tiles on the other wall.

INSTALLING WALL TILE
continued

Install cut tiles before the mastic on the wall has started to harden. If it has skinned over, the tiles will not stick; carefully scrape the mastic off the wall, and butter the back of each cut tile before installing.

INSTALL CUT TILES: Measure for each cut tile; do not assume that all the tiles in a row will be the same size. Cut tiles carefully so that they fit fairly tightly but not so tightly that you have to force them in—that can cause adjoining tiles to shift. Don't assume that grout or caulk will cover the joint on an inside corner where there is tile on both walls. Take the extra time and throw out tiles that are a bit too narrow. If they are slightly too wide, rub the cut edge with a rubbing stone (see *page 53*).

GROUT, CLEAN, AND CAULK

Allow the mastic to set for at least 24 hours. (In humid conditions, it might take longer.) To test whether the tiles have set, try to slide a tile along the wall with your hand. If it moves, the mastic has not fully set. Clean away mastic on the tile surface, as well as any mastic that has welled up between the tiles.

APPLY GROUT: If the grout joints are $\frac{1}{8}$ inch wide or wider, use sanded grout. Unsanded grout is fine for narrower joints. Mix grout with latex additive; if you mix with water, the grout will probably crack. Aim for the consistency of toothpaste. Let it set for 10 minutes (called "slaking"), then mix it again.

Apply the grout in two steps. First, press it into the joints by spreading diagonally across the grout lines with the grout float held nearly flat. Work in at least two directions. Next, tilt the float up and scrape away as much excess grout as possible. Look carefully for voids in the grout, and fill them.

You can shape the joints with a striking tool, but many people find that they can do this just as well with a sponge.

CLEAN THE TILES: Wipe the surface with a damp sponge. Rinse the sponge in clean water every few minutes. Clean two or three times. As you clean, wipe the grout lines to bring them to consistent depth and texture. Allow the surface to dry, then buff away the haze with a clean, dry cloth.

CAULK: Wait a day for the grout to set, then caulk the inside corners, following the techniques shown on the opposite page.

INSTALLING MOSAIC SHEETS

Rubber mallet

Mosaic tiles come attached to sheets ready for installation. After applying the mastic (see *page 25*), press the mosaic sheet straight into the mastic without sliding it. Smooth it with the back of your hand. (Take special care to set the sheet correctly—if you slide it into place, not only will the tiles adhere poorly, you will also have a lot of mastic to clean off.) Tap a scrap of plywood over the surface with a rubber mallet to make sure each tile is embedded in the mastic. As you place subsequent sheets of tile, make sure the seams are tight: The surest sign of an amateur job is a telltale gap.

To cut off whole tiles, simply cut the paper or fabric backing with a utility knife. Cut individual tiles with a snap cutter, and place each one individually.

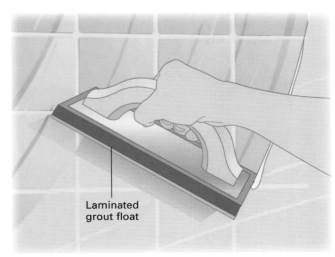

A laminated grout float works like a squeegee, scraping the tiles nearly clean. Scrape diagonally across the grout lines so the float does not dig into the grout joints.

Wipe the surface at least two times with a dampened sponge, taking care to maintain even grout joints. After the grout dries, buff to a high shine with a dry cloth.

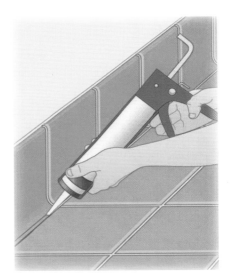

Practice caulking until you can lay a clean bead. You may simply apply the caulk with a tube, or you may have to wipe away the excess with your finger. Dampen your finger with mineral spirits first.

To ensure a clean caulk bead, lay down two strips of masking tape, apply the caulk, then pull the tape away.

Masking tape

MOUNTING ACCESSORIES

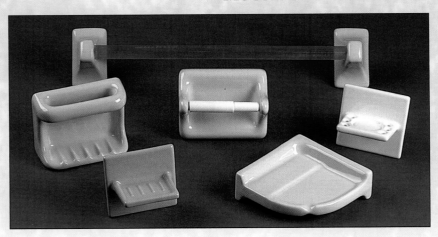

Surface-mounted soap dishes, toothpaste holders, and some other accessories mount directly onto tiles; recessed accessories are mounted to the wall before the tiles are set.

Either way, set the accessory using an adhesive that is stronger than standard organic mastic used for wall tile. You can use thin-set mortar, epoxy mortar, or epoxy adhesive. Use strips of masking tape to hold the accessory in place until the adhesive has set fully. Apply caulk or grout to the joint between the accessory and the tiles.

TILING A TUB SURROUND

Tiling around a tub and shower area is an affordable project that can dramatically improve your bathroom. Because tubs are often slightly off-kilter, your greatest challenge will be laying out and cutting the tiles along the rim of the tub.

PREPARING AND LAYING OUT

Remove the faucet handles and the spout. Wrap the shower head arm with masking tape to protect it. Cover the tub as you would for removing tiles (see *page 42*).

If you are replacing old tiles, remove them (see *page 42*), scrape the wall clean or install new backerboard, and scrape the top edge of the tub completely clean of old caulk and grout. If you are installing new backerboard (see *pages 43–45*), set it about ¼ inch above the tub ledge.

Check the tub for level on all three sides. If it is perfect, you can start with a row of full tiles resting on the tub. If not, lay out the first row for tiles about three-quarters wide (see *page 56*), and start laying tiles with the next row up. Walls around a shower are usually tiled either to 6 inches or so above the showerhead or all the way to the ceiling.

Place a horizontal row of tiles around the tub ledge to determine your layout lines. Mark a vertical line near the middle of the back wall, and either draw a horizontal line or attach a straight board for a batten. At the side walls, you may need to start your layout with the outside edge, especially if it ends at an outside corner (see *page 57*).

SETTING THE TILES

Many professional installers prefer thin-set mortar for a tub surround because it is more resistant to water than organic mastic. However, thin-set does not grab the tiles as well as mastic, so the tiles may slide. Also, mastic—unlike thin-set—allows you to adjust

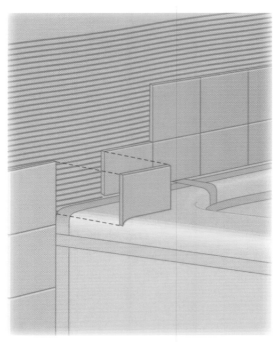

The tile at the tub's corner is tricky to cut properly but is critical to the appearance of the job.

Cover a tub tightly before working on it, but leave just a little bit of the ledge exposed so you can set tiles on it. Establish layout lines for all three sides with dry runs of tile.

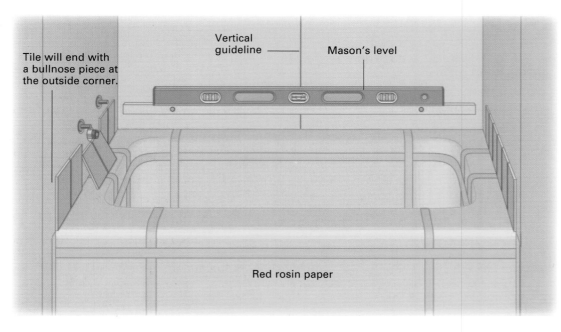

Tile will end with a bullnose piece at the outside corner.

Vertical guideline

Mason's level

Red rosin paper

tile positions for 10 or 20 minutes after setting them. If a wall is kept properly grouted and sealed, tile set with organic mastic will last for decades.

INSTALL THE TILES: Apply adhesive with a notched trowel, taking care not to cover the layout lines or to go beyond the area to be tiled. Install all the full tiles, including the bullnose tiles and the corners, then fill in the edges with cut tiles. If you started with a batten, remove it and install the bottom row of tiles. Cut the bottom tiles to leave a gap of about ⅛ inch above the tub ledge.

Notches or holes around pipes do not have to be precise; in fact, tile should not touch any pipe. Make sure, however, that the spout or flange will cover the cutout.

At the front ends of the tub, at least one vertical row of tile should extend down to the floor. The tile at each top corner of the tub requires a curved cut. Make a cardboard template to mark a tile for cutting. Cut with a rod saw (see *pages 52–53*). Take your time; it may take several tries to get it right. This piece is so visible that the job will look sloppy if it is not cut precisely.

GROUT AND CLEAN THE TILES: Grout is an important first defense that keeps water away from your substrate. Apply the grout with a laminated grout float (see *page 59*),

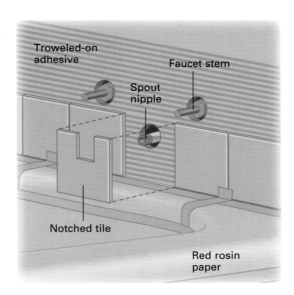

Troweled-on adhesive

Faucet stem

Spout nipple

Notched tile

Red rosin paper

Use a rod saw, wet saw, or nibbling tool to cut notches for pipes. Make sure that the spout or the handle flange will cover the gap.

being careful so no voids occur in the grout joints. To remove excess grout, wipe the surface several times with a dampened sponge rinsed in clean water. Let the surface dry. As a final step, buff the surface with a clean cloth.

Reattach the plumbing, such as the shower handles and the spout, taking care not to scratch them. Wrap the spout with tape or cloth before tightening it with a wrench.

WINDOW TREATMENTS

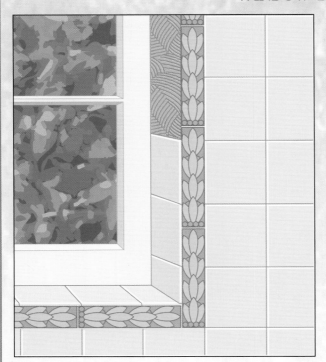

Many old homes built before shower and tub combinations were common feature a wood window in the rear wall of a tub surround. It's a notorious trouble spot. Water from the shower can quickly rot wood sashes and trim.

If the window itself is rotting, you could replace it with a vinyl window or have a mason install glass block with a vent panel.

Whether you replace the window or not, it makes sense to tear off the casing, then tile over the recess. If the jamb is in good shape, tile over it. If not, remove it and install strips of backerboard. At the bottom, shim up the back edge of the backerboard slightly so water will run off away from the window.

Tile the wall up to the edges of the recess; you may want to end with border tiles, as shown here. Then, install bullnose tiles in the recess to cover the edges of the wall tile. Tile the top edge of the recess first; you may have to support these tiles with a board and two braces until the adhesive sets. Set the rest of the bullnose tiles so that the grout lines match up.

Allow the adhesive to set, then grout the tile. Caulk the joint between the recess tiles and the window so no water can seep in.

BATHROOM SINK

The sink and countertop here are unified in appearance with the surrounding walls. If your countertop does not abut the walls, install edging pieces at the sides.

Lend a custom look to your bathroom by tiling the counter around a built-in sink. For a uniform appearance and easy cleaning, continue the tile onto the walls.
BUILD THE SUBSTRATE: Remove the top from an existing cabinet base, purchase and install a new vanity cabinet, or build one from scratch. Construct the top with ¾-inch plywood, then install plastic sheeting and ½-inch cement backerboard.

Choose an enamel bathroom sink that harmonizes with your tiles. Then, cut the hole in the top for the sink (see *pages 76–78*).

To add a ledge like the one shown, build a simple frame of pressure-treated 2×4s, fastened together with screws. Lay plastic sheeting over the frame, then cover it with ½-inch cement backerboard. Cut these small pieces carefully, and smooth all the edges with a rubbing stone. Design the ledge so you can lay as many full tiles on it as possible.
LAY THEM OUT: Tile the walls first (see *pages 54–59*), the countertop next, and the ledge last. When planning the layout of the wall tiles, consider where the countertop and ledge will go; you may or may not want to line up grout lines. Lay out to avoid narrow slivers of tile.

Lay out the countertop so it is symmetrical, with cut tiles of the same size at both ends. Finish the front with V-cap or bullnose tile. (Wood edging is not a good idea because the bathroom is often moist for long periods.) Set all the uncut tiles in a dry run to make sure of the layout. (See *pages 80 to 81* for specifics on installing tile edging.)
SET AND GROUT THE TILES: Tile the walls as explained on *pages 54 to 59*. Then, spread thin-set mortar over the countertop with a notched trowel, and set the tiles in it. Place plastic spacers between tiles to maintain consistent grout joints. Set the edging and the field tiles at the same time, and align them evenly. Set the full tiles, then the cut ones. Tap with a beater block to bed the tiles and level the surface.

Framing for a ledge like this can be a plan-as-you-go process. As you assemble the pieces, check to see that you will not end up with too-narrow tiles anywhere.

On the ledge, set the full tiles first, including the bullnose pieces. Then cut and install the tiles that require straight cuts. Make sure all these tiles are correctly aligned and spaced, then measure for the tiles that will be cut at angles. Some of these are complicated and may take several attempts. It may help to make a cardboard template for each one.

Grout the entire installation at once (see *pages 58–59*). Where the countertop and the ledge meet the wall, apply caulk instead of grout. (See *page 59* for tips on caulking tile joints.)

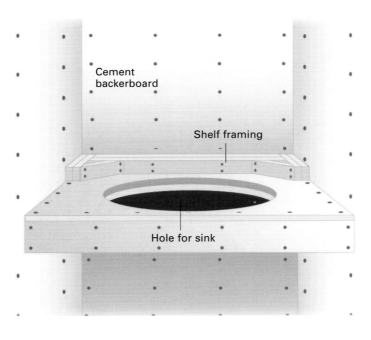

Cement backerboard

Shelf framing

Hole for sink

KITCHEN BACKSPLASH

Evenly spaced decorative tiles combine with border tiles to give this backsplash a sense of order. This surface will be easier to keep clean than a painted or wallpapered wall or a wood backsplash.

Whether you lay one course of tile along the wall behind a countertop or cover the entire wall between counter and cabinets, tile makes an ideal backsplash. Not only will it stand up to the splashes and spatters of cooking, it can add a striking decorative touch as well.

DESIGN OPTIONS: If your countertop is tiled, you may want to cover the backsplash with matching tiles. You could sprinkle a few decorative tiles in the layout or add a border strip about halfway up to match a tile border on the edge of the countertop. So they'll be clearly visible, place decorative elements at least 6 inches below a wall cabinet.

LAYING OUT: The wall between a countertop and a wall cabinet is usually about 18 inches tall. Wherever the backsplash will not butt up against a wall cabinet, install bullnose pieces along the top (see *page 57*).

In the examples shown on this page, large tiles are set on-point at a 45-degree angle. Begin this kind of layout by snapping a chalk line for the bottom border strip parallel with the countertop surface, and set the border tiles. Then measure and mark the wall with the layout for the larger angled tiles.

If you are tiling only one wall, arrange the layout so the end tiles are the same width. If you need to tile around a corner, as shown, carefully line up the tiles from both walls so they meet correctly in the corner.

Position a tile on the wall at a 45-degree angle, its bottom corner a grout-width above the border tiles. Carefully measure from the top of the border tile and the two outer corners of the on-point tile. On each wall, draw or snap a horizontal layout line that distance above the border tiles.

CUTTING AND SETTING THE TILES: In this design, you will need quite a few triangular tiles, square ones cut precisely from corner to corner. A snap cutter will help you mass-produce these (see *page 52*).

Start at the inside corner, lining up all tiles so they match, then work outward. Follow the general tiling and grouting techniques for walls, described on *pages 54 to 59*.

Start laying out and setting tiles at the most critical point— in this case, an inside corner. If you can cut tiles perfectly in half, installing the rest of the tiles will be easy.

Chalk line

Tile 45° on point

INSTALLING FLOOR TILE

Before tiling, be sure your floor is strong enough not to flex and crack the tiles and that the surface is smooth and free of waves. (For how to firm up a floor, see *pages 34 and 35*; for how to smooth and level a floor, see *pages 36–38*.) Choose only strong tiles designed for use on a floor (see *pages 22 and 23*), and set them in thin-set mortar mixed with latex additive (see *page 49*).

LAYING OUT THE FLOOR

Layout is a dress rehearsal for your final installation. It's when you make choices about where each tile will be positioned and how to arrange tiles to minimize cuts.

Most rooms are out of square, so you may have to run the tiles parallel to one wall or lay out the tiles so they run slightly out of parallel to two walls. Laying them out will help avoid unsightly slivers.

There's one place in every room where the tile will be most visible and other spots where it will barely show. For example, you may want to center bathroom tiles between the tub and the vanity, since any narrow tiles behind the toilet won't be obvious. However, in a front entryway with no obstructions, a symmetrical installation will probably look best.

Layout is often a matter of trial and error. Your first attempt may have slivers in the wrong place. Try new arrangements until you find the one that looks best, requires the fewest cuts, and places compromises where they are least likely to be noticed.

CHECK WALLS FOR SQUARE: You cannot tell whether walls are square by holding a framing square in the corner—the walls may splay out beyond the ends of the square. Check them by laying a full sheet of drywall or plywood in the corner. Factory ends and edges on full sheets are square. The 3-4-5 triangle method is another way to check for square. To do this, mark one wall 3 feet from the corner and the adjacent one 4 feet from the corner. If the diagonal distance between the two marks is exactly 5 feet, then the wall is square.

Also, check for waves in the wall. They may not be noticeable unless you place the edge of a sheet of plywood next to the wall or snap a chalk line on the floor.

If a room is out of square or has a wavy wall, think through your layout carefully. You may choose to have one row of edge tiles that visibly increases in size along its length, positioned where it will not be noticeable (perhaps under a couch). Or, you may decide to install two or more edge rows that are only slightly imperfect.

LAY OUT ON GRAPH PAPER: If your layout is at all complicated, make a scale sketch on graph paper. Measure your tiles, taking into account the grout joints. To check for accuracy, line up five tiles with spacers, measure, and divide by five. Let each square on the graph paper equal one tile, with grout joints on two adjacent sides.

A full sheet of plywood and the 3-4-5 triangle method are two good ways to check a wall for square.

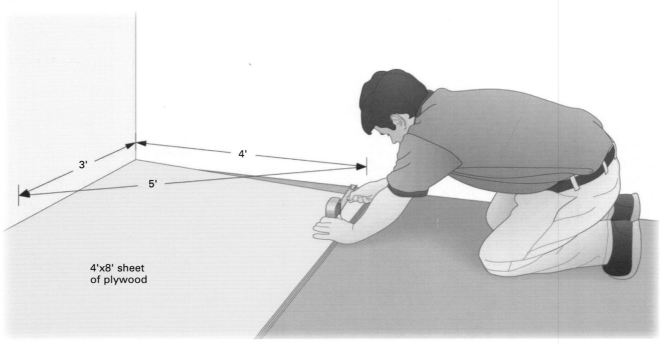

3'

4'

5'

4'x8' sheet of plywood

Draw an outline of the room to this scale, indicating exactly how far out of square the walls are. Experiment with different layouts until you have a plan that eliminates—or at least minimizes—the number of slivers.

SET TILES IN A DRY RUN: If you have a simple rectangular room, lay the tiles on the floor, spaced as they will be in the finished installation. Once the tiles are in place, you can see whether you need to make adjustments to avoid slivers.

MAKE A JURY STICK: A jury stick allows you to skip some measuring and calculating so you can quickly make layout decisions. If your floor is more complicated than a rectangle, take a few minutes to make one.

To make one, lay about 10 or so tiles on the floor, spaced as they will be in the finished installation. Lay a straight board, 6 to 8 feet long, next to the tiles, and draw marks on the board at the center of each grout joint.

Placing the jury stick on the floor accomplishes the same thing as laying tiles in a dry run, but does it much more quickly. The disadvantage for a do-it-yourselfer is that you can get confused after you have moved the stick several times. If you feel you are losing your way, set tiles on the floor in a dry run.

FIGURING TILE NEEDS

After you've mapped your layout by using graph paper, a dry run, or a jury stick, you can easily calculate how many tiles you will need. For a rectangular room, multiply the number of tiles used for the length times the number for the width. Be sure to include all the cut tiles.

For a more complicated layout, you can count the tiles if you made a graph-paper sketch. Or divide the job into rectangles, and figure the number of tiles for each rectangle. Then add up the totals for all the rectangles.

If you are unsure, take dimensioned drawings of your installation to your tile dealer for help figuring the square footage and the approximate number of tiles needed.

Order 10 percent more tile than you need. Everybody makes mistakes in calculating and cutting tile. Save some of the leftover tiles for future repairs—they may be hard to find years later. You can usually return unused tiles for a refund, too.

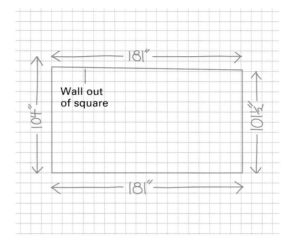

A graph-paper drawing helps you visualize a layout and adjust the positions of tiles.

Wall out of square

181"

40"

10½"

181"

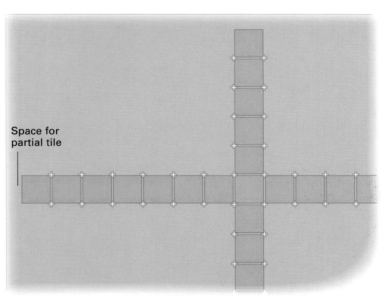

Space for partial tile

Laying tiles in a dry run is a bit tedious, but it is the surest way to visualize what the finished tile job will look like.

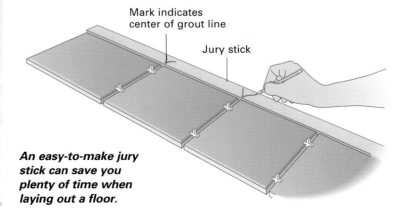

Mark indicates center of grout line

Jury stick

An easy-to-make jury stick can save you plenty of time when laying out a floor.

INSTALLING FLOOR TILE
continued

SPACING IRREGULAR TILES

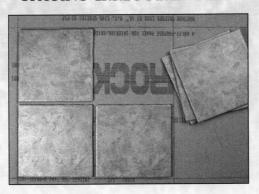

When setting slightly irregular tiles, such as Mexican pavers, you cannot rely on spacers or a batten to line up straight rows. But you do want the floor to display a generally consistent pattern of tiles. The grid method described here can accomplish that.

After you have figured the layout and marked layout lines on the floor, draw a grid pattern on the floor, with each square sized to contain either four (2×2) or nine (3×3) tiles. For instance, you might draw 24-inch squares, each containing nine 7¾-inch tiles.

With a helper, mark the grid lines with a chalk line. Be careful not to erase the lines while you work.

Trowel thin-set inside the square, and set the tiles in place. Stand up and view the arrangement from different angles. Adjust tiles until they look like they have consistent joints.

DRAW REFERENCE LINES: The first lines you draw or chalk on the floor establish the orientation of the tile job, rather than actual tile positions. In a square room, reference lines are easy: Just draw straight, square lines about a foot from the walls, using a sheet of plywood or the 3-4-5 triangle method.

If the room is not square, draw lines all the way around the room, square to each other and about a foot away from each wall. At least one of these lines will not be parallel to its adjacent wall, depending on the choices you made when you figured the layout.

MARK LAYOUT LINES: These lines indicate exactly where the first tiles will be laid. Align them perfectly parallel to the reference lines, and place them according to the calculations you made with a dry run, jury stick, or graph paper. Place the layout lines near the center of the room so you can start tiling there and work outward. Draw at least two perpendicular lines, one running the full length of the room and one the full width.

LAYOUT FOR AN L-SHAPED ROOM: This is usually not much more difficult than a single rectangular room; just think of the room as two rectangles. Mark a pair of perpendicular reference lines running the length and width of each rectangle, then draw layout lines with a dry run, jury stick, or graph-paper drawing to make sure you have no slivers along the walls. Often an L-shaped room calls for some compromises to accommodate the six walls.

LAYOUT FOR TWO ROOMS JOINED BY A DOORWAY: Treat them as if they were one big room, and lay them both out at the same

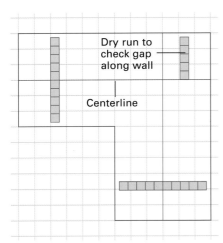

When laying out for an L-shaped room, pay attention to how tiles will fit against all six walls.

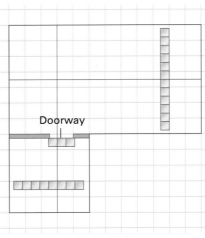

When two rooms adjoin, try to center tiles in the doorway—one of the most visible spots in the room.

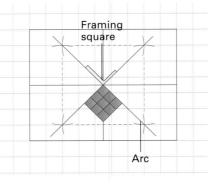

When tiling at an angle, draw perpendicular lines across the length and width of the room. Then draw arcs equidistant from their junction. Lines drawn through the arc intersections and center will be at 45-degree angles to the original lines.

time. Because the doorway is a focal point, it's best to center the tiles there, with tiles cut to the same size on both sides. You may not be able to do this without having slivers along one or more walls.

LAYOUT FOR DIAGONAL TILES: Begin by checking the room for square and drawing reference lines, just as for an ordinary tile job. Based on the reference lines, draw perpendicular lines running the length and width of the room, in the exact center of it.

From the intersection of the two lines (the exact center of the room), measure out an equal distance in both directions along each line. Draw marks at those four points. Drive a nail partway into one of the four marks.

Tie a pencil to one end of a mason's line (regular string will stretch), and wrap the other end around the nail. Adjust the line so that the pencil tip touches the centerpoint of the room. Hold the pencil perpendicular to the layout line, and draw an arc; do the same on the opposite side of the line. Pull out the nail and repeat the procedure for the other three marks (see drawing on the *opposite page*).

You now have four sets of intersecting arcs. Snap two chalk lines through the intersections of the arcs and the centerpoint. Check that these lines are perpendicular to each other, using a framing square. These are the layout lines for the diagonal tiles.

Lay the tiles in a dry run to determine if there will be tiny triangles at any wall. If so, adjust the layout lines. (You don't have to repeat the complicated process described above; just draw new lines parallel to the old ones.)

Laying diagonal tiles is especially tricky in rooms that turn corners or have obstructions, such as cabinets. In those instances, draw initial layout lines and dry-lay tiles extending in several directions, as shown (*above right*).

PUT DOWN BATTENS: To align the first rows of tile, nail or screw long, straight boards, called battens, against your layout lines. Check to make sure they form a precise right angle. Press the tiles against the battens when you lay them.

For a reliably straight batten, cut a strip of plywood, and place the factory edge (see *page 64*) against the layout line. If you are installing tile on a concrete floor and cannot easily screw the batten down, hold it in place with heavy weights. Check occasionally during the tiling to make sure the batten hasn't moved.

Laying out diagonal tiles in a meandering room can get complicated. Take the time to do a dry run that tests all walls.

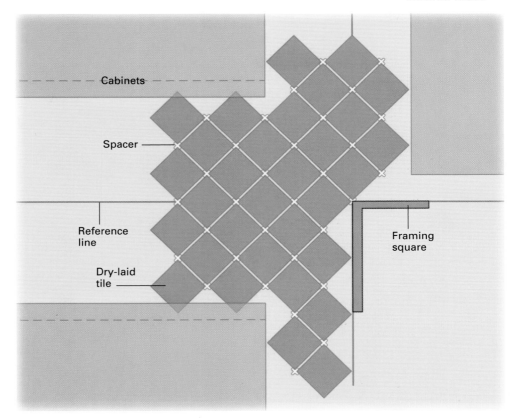

Cabinets

Spacer

Reference line

Dry-laid tile

Framing square

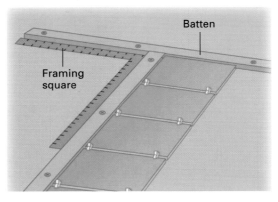

Batten

Framing square

Battens attached to the floor make it easy to lay the first rows of tile in perfect alignment

INSTALLING FLOOR TILE
continued

SETTING THE TILE

Plan the order in which you will tile the floor so you don't tile yourself into a corner. If you want to set all the tiles in one day—including the cut tiles along the walls and at doorways—install the cut tiles as you go. This way, you won't have to step on tiles recently set in mortar. On a large floor, you may decide to set all the full tiles in one day, then cut and install edge tiles a day or two later.

MIX THE THIN-SET: Fill a 5-gallon bucket about ⅓ full of thin-set powder. Pour in enough latex additive to barely moisten the powder, and stir the mixture with a stiff scraper or a piece of 1×2. Gradually add more liquid until the thin-set is about the consistency of toothpaste.

The thin-set must be wet enough for the tiles to stick to, but not so runny that it flows. To test the consistency, spread a small amount with a notched trowel; the ridges should maintain their shape, not slump flat.

Mixing by hand is arduous. If you have a lot of mixing to do, rent a heavy-duty ½-inch drill and a large mixing paddle. Fill the bucket half full of thin-set powder and add latex liquid. Firmly wedge the bucket between your feet to keep it from rotating as you mix (see *page 49*).

SPREAD THE THIN-SET: Spread only as much thin-set as you can tile over in 10 minutes or so. (The time will vary greatly, depending on humidity and how stiff the mixture is.) If the thin-set sits too long on the

floor before you tile, it will skin over and the tiles will not adhere. Start with a small area—about 2 feet square—and work up to larger areas as you get used to tiling.

Spread the thin-set with a square-notched trowel recommended for your tile. Most tiles call for a trowel with ¼-inch by ¼-inch or ¼-inch by ⅜-inch notches. Scoop out and plop down several trowelfuls of thin-set. Spread it first with the straight side of the trowel, holding the trowel fairly flat to push the thin-set across the floor. Then spread with the notched side of the trowel, tipping the trowel to about 45 degrees. Maintain the angle consistently to keep the adhesive thickness uniform. Scrape away blobs by troweling again. Do not cover up your layout lines.

Some thick tiles and those with deep ridges on the back need extra thin-set. After spreading adhesive on the floor, butter tile backs with thin-set, using the same trowel.

SET WHOLE TILES: Place each tile in place, and give it a slight twist. Don't slide a tile into place: Sliding can make the bed of thin-set uneven in thickness.

Align the tiles along a layout line or batten, or slip in plastic spacers at all four

Rubber mallet

Beater block

CHECK YOUR THIN-SET

Even if you press tiles firmly into thin-set, they may not actually be sticking. Every once in a while, pick up a representative tile and examine its back. Nearly the entire surface should be coated with thin-set. Large gaps indicate that the tiles are not really set; they might work loose after a while.

If the thin-set is not sticking, it may be too dry. Or you may have waited too long after troweling it before setting the tile. If a section of thin-set has skinned over or has begun to harden, scrape it up and throw it away; it cannot be reused.

corners. You can adjust tile positions as long as the thin-set remains wet. If you move tiles after thin-set has begun to harden, the tile may not stick to the floor. Avoid walking on tiles you have laid. If you must step on them, lay a sheet of plywood over the tiles first.

BED THE TILES: Tap the tiles into place every 10 to 15 minutes with a hammer or mallet and a beater block made of 2×6 or 2×4 wrapped with a piece of towel or carpeting. This bedding process guarantees a sure bond of the tile to the thin-set and helps keep the surface level.

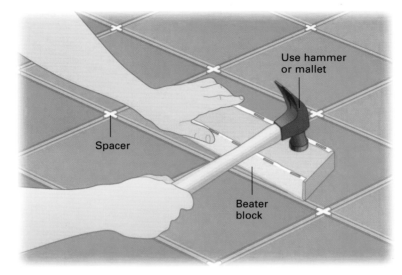

Tap with a beater block to make sure the tiles are bonding with the thin-set, and to help maintain a level surface.

Run a straightedge across the tiles from time to time to check for high or low tiles. If a tile is high, tap it down with the beater block. If it won't go down, there may be a shard of tile or other obstruction on the floor. Remove the tile, scrape the area, and apply adhesive again. If a tile lies below the level of its neighbors, pry it up, apply thin-set, and reset it.

KEEP THE TILES CLEAN: This job can get messy, especially if you have to reset tiles. Thin-set is much more difficult to clean off when it has set, so keep a damp sponge at the ready, and wipe up any blobs or streaks immediately. Rinse the sponge often. Keep your hands clean, and wipe off the trowel handle if you get thin-set on it.

If you'll be installing cut tiles the day after you set the field tiles, scrape away excess thin-set from the floor where they'll be placed.

MEASURE TILES FOR CUTTING: Floor tiles usually do not have to be cut precisely, as long as the cut edges will be covered by molding or a threshold. (For tile-cutting techniques, see *pages 52–53*.)

Use another tile instead of a tape measure to mark a tile for cutting. Place the tile to be trimmed directly on top of the full tile that's next to the gap to be filled. Place another full tile on top, and slide it against the wall. Then, guide on the back edge of the top tile to mark the cutting line. Cut the tile shorter than this line by the thickness of two grout lines—one on each side of the cut tile.

To mark an L-shaped tile at an outside corner, follow the same method to draw lines in both directions (see drawing *at right*).

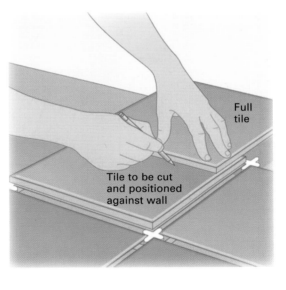

Use a second tile to measure and mark for a cut tile. Take into account the thickness of the grout joints.

To measure for a cutout at a corner, use a second tile to mark both of the cut lines.

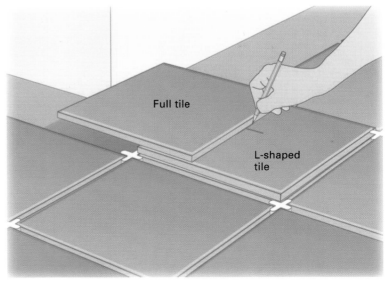

INSTALLING FLOOR TILE
continued

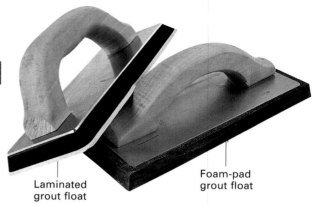

Laminated grout float

Foam-pad grout float

GROUTING

Applying grout is an important step that will make or break your tile installation. Grout lines that aren't consistent in depth and shape will look sloppy, and gaps in the grout can allow moisture to penetrate to the substrate. Grouting takes a surprising amount of time. Allow plenty of time for a good job.

PREPARING FOR GROUTING: If you used plastic spacers, pry them out with a screwdriver or awl. Some tilers leave the spacers in, but the shallower grout over the spacers may dry to a slightly different color. It might chip away in time, too.

Pry spacers out of the corners with a screwdriver, taking care not to scratch the tile. A scrubbing tool with stiff plastic webbing is ideal for cleaning away excess thin-set.

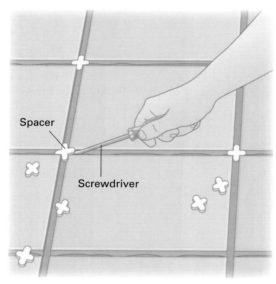

Spacer

Screwdriver

Once the spacers are out, clean away any thin-set on the tile surface. Also, scrape away any thin-set that has welled up between the tiles with a screwdriver or grout saw. The cavities between the tiles should be deep enough to allow a grout depth of at least ¼ inch at all points.

MIX THE GROUT: Use sanded grout made for floor tile. How much you need depends on the size of the tiles, the width of the grout lines, and the area of the floor. Your tile dealer can tell you how much to buy.

Follow the grout manufacturer's mixing instructions. With certain types, you must mix an entire box to ensure consistent color. If you have the option of mixing with water or latex liquid, use latex. The grout will be stronger and more resistant to cracking and flaking.

Grout should be stiff enough that it doesn't quite pour out of a bucket; you should have to shake the bucket a bit to get it to move.

Push the grout firmly into the joints, holding the float nearly flat and moving it back and forth. Check that all the joints are filled, leaving no voids.

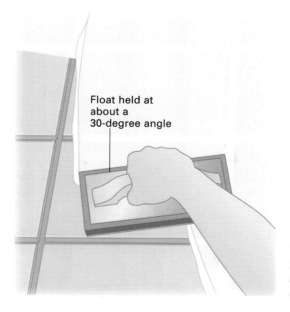

Float held at about a 30-degree angle

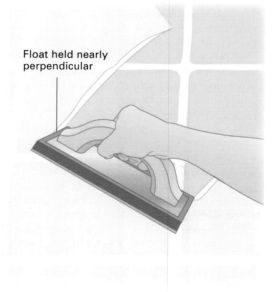

Float held nearly perpendicular

Tip the laminated float up to scrape away nearly all the excess grout from the tile surface. Work systematically so you don't end up with occasional blobs of grout.

It should hold its shape and not sag. Mix the grout to a toothpaste-like consistency, stirring it with a firm trowel or stick. Then allow it to slake (or set) for 10 minutes. This will stiffen it a bit, but it will loosen up again when you remix it. If it remains too stiff, add more liquid.

APPLY THE GROUT: Start in one corner and work outward. Dump or scoop out a small mound of grout onto the floor. Hold the grout float at about a 30-degree angle—nearly flat—and push the grout into the joints. Spread it with sweeping motions diagonally across the tiles. Make two or three passes, each in a different direction, to make sure you have packed the grout firmly into all the joints.

SCRAPE IT AWAY: Here is where a laminated grout float, which acts like a squeegee, has a big advantage over a foam-pad float. Tilt the laminated float up at about a right angle to the floor, and wipe the tiles nearly clean. Hold the float diagonally to the joint lines so the float edge doesn't dig into the joint. If you accidentally gouge away grout from a joint, refill it immediately and scrape again. Work systematically: A thorough squeegeeing will save work when it comes time to clean.

CLEAN AND FINISH THE JOINTS: To avoid diluting and weakening the grout, clean the floor with as little water as possible.

On a large floor, the towel method works best for the first cleaning (see *above right*). Soak a large towel in water, and wring it out so it is damp. Spread it on the floor, and pull it slowly toward you to remove most of the excess grout from the tile surfaces.

Then, use a large, damp sponge for most of the cleaning and tooling. (You can purchase special tools for producing even joint lines, but the simplest method is to shape the joints with your sponge as you clean the floor.) First wipe the floor in circular motions. Rinse out the sponge often. Then wipe along the grout lines to produce joints that are consistent in depth. Repeat two or three times, until the tiles are clean and the joints all look perfect.

BUFF AND SEAL: Allow the grout to dry for several hours. Then, buff the surface with a dry cloth to remove the haze and brighten the tile surface. Two or three weeks after applying the grout, apply a penetrating sealer or impregnator recommended by your tile dealer. If the tile is porous, seal it for easier cleaning. Apply grout sealer with a small foam brush; use a foam paint roller on tiles.

Damp towel · Clean water · Sponge

Dragging a large, damp towel across a floor can clean a large area quickly. Use it once on one side, then flip it over and drag again. Rinse thoroughly when it is dirty on both sides. Or, wipe the surface gently with a sponge so you don't disturb the grout lines. Then use the sponge to form grout joints that are consistently deep.

USING A GROUT BAG

Grout bag

Use a grout bag in difficult-to-reach joints or where tiles are so porous that they would soak up grout if you applied it with a standard grout float. It resembles a cake-decorating bag; you apply grout directly into the joints so that very little grout spills onto the tile. When you buy the bag, purchase a tip made for your joint width. Mix the grout as you normally would, and pour it into the bag. Press the tip into the joint, and squeeze the bag as you fill the joints. After the grout has begun to harden, shape it with a joint tool to make consistent joints. After it has hardened further, sweep the joints with a stiff brush. Avoid using a wet sponge; that would spread the grout out onto the tiles.

FINISHING TOUCHES

Once the floor tile is installed and grouted, exposed edges of the tiles along the baseboard and at doorway thresholds need to be covered. You must also reinstall the toilet, sinks, and any other fixtures you removed. If a pipe runs through the floor tile, caulk around it and install a split flange made for that size of pipe (see *page 48*). Wait a day or two for the grout to dry thoroughly before taking care of these finishing touches.

BASEBOARDS

Where the wall meets the tiled floor, finish the job with bullnose tiles, wood molding, or vinyl cove base.

BULLNOSE TILE: This method is attractive, but it's fairly expensive and the tiles can be difficult to install. You can purchase bullnose tiles of either the same size and color as the floor tiles or a contrasting size and material. (With the latter, you won't have to worry about lining up the grout lines.)

Even carefully laid floor tiles rarely are perfectly level, so you will probably have to adjust some to achieve a straight edge along the top of the baseboard tiles. Start by leaning the bullnose tiles against the wall in a dry run. Place spacers between the tiles and under them. Line them up so their grout lines match those on the floor. Cut pieces for the corners.

Place the baseboard tiles on the floor near where they will go, and chalk or draw a line on the wall about ½ inch below where the top of the baseboard tiles will be. Have wood shims of various thicknesses on hand, then apply thin-set or organic mastic to the wall with a small notched trowel, being careful not to go above the line.

Press the tiles into the adhesive, using the spacers. After you have set several feet of tiles, check the top edge with a level or straightedge. If one or more tiles is out of alignment, remove a spacer or two at the bottom and install a wood shim that is just thick enough to bring the tile into alignment. Make these adjustments before the adhesive hardens.

Allow the adhesive to dry, and caulk the bottom edge. If you grout this joint, it may crack (see *page 48*). When the caulk has dried, grout to the vertical joint lines.

WOOD MOLDING: If you removed base molding or base shoe before tiling the floor (see *page 40*), sand and paint it before reinstalling it. If the base molding or base shoe is cracked or has an unattractive alligator-skin surface, purchase new molding, then prime and paint it before installing.

For a tight-fit at inside corners, use a coped joint (see *left*). To do that, cut the first piece square and install it tightly against

Use spacers under and between baseboard tiles to maintain grout lines of the same width as those on the floor.

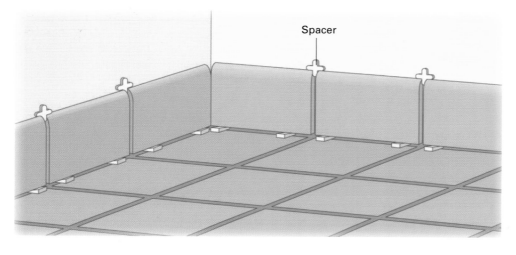

Spacer

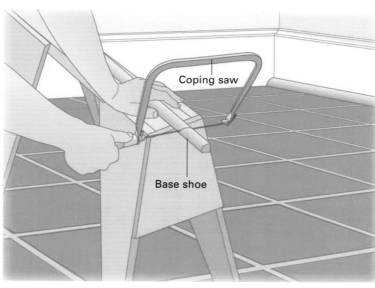

Coping saw

Base shoe

A coped joint will fit tightly even if the walls are not square to each other. Cut the second piece at a 45-degree angle, then use a coping saw to cut the profile.

the wall. Cut the second piece at a 45-degree angle, then cut its profile with a coping saw, which can cut tight curves. The coped cut will fit tightly over the other piece.

VINYL COVE BASE: This is inexpensive, quick to install, easy to keep clean, and available in a variety of colors. You can buy cove base in 4-foot-long pieces; several widths are available. Buy special corner pieces for outside corners.

Apply cove base adhesive to the wall, using a special notched trowel of the correct width. Set the cove base firmly into the adhesive, and press it into the adhesive with a small roller or the heel of your hand to make sure it sticks securely.

At an inside corner, cut the first piece square and install it tightly to the adjoining wall. On the second piece, cut the bottom portion—just the part where it flares outward—at a 45-degree angle. Dry-test to make sure it fits tightly.

Apply cove base adhesive evenly so that the cove base will adhere completely and no adhesive will squeeze out onto the floor or the wall. Use a utility knife and a square to cut the cove base to fit.

THRESHOLDS

Your tiled floor will probably be higher than an adjoining floor. Choose a threshold that bridges the different floor levels attractively and neatly.

FLUSH THRESHOLDS: A piece that rests between the two floor surfaces makes the smoothest transition. Because it lies flush with both surfaces, there are no lips for people to trip over and no crannies to trap dirt. A flush threshold can be difficult to install because both the tile and the adjoining floor must be straight-edged and parallel to each other.

You may be able to custom-make a wood flush threshold. Purchase a standard threshold or a piece of lumber that is wider than you need and thick enough to fit flush with the highest floor surface. Cut it to length, and rip-cut it to the correct width. Bevel one edge with a plane or a belt sander.

Your tile center may sell a threshold made of marble or stone that matches your tile. Order it beveled so it fits flush with both surfaces, or add a narrow piece of molding to make the transition to the lower floor level.

SURFACE THRESHOLDS: These are the simplest to install. Silver- or brass-colored metal thresholds are available in several widths; most are beveled to fit between

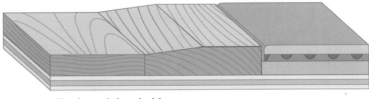

Hardwood threshold

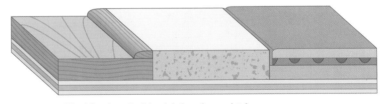

Marble threshold with hardwood trim

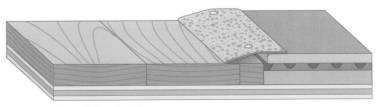

Metal threshold

different floor levels. Cut one of these to length with tin snips or a hacksaw, and attach it by driving in the nails provided.

If you are tiling up to a wood threshold at an exterior door, you may be able to lift the threshold and slip the tiles under it. Or, remove the old threshold and install a new one. You'll probably need to cut the door after doing this.

In addition to these threshold possibilities, your tile dealer may have other options that complement both your tiles and your adjoining wood or carpeted floor.

Labels in top illustration: Vinyl cove base · Adhesive applied with notched trowel · Roller

FLOOR TILE DESIGN OPTIONS

A design like this does not need to be a prescribed size, because the interior angled tiles can be cut to fit.

One of the many advantages of tile is the ability to adapt patterns to suit almost any room. Randomly sprinkling decorative tiles works well on walls, but floors call for symmetrical patterns centered in the room.

There are no set rules, but designs like this should cover from one quarter to one half the total area of the room so the design will neither dominate the room nor look lost in it. A design should more or less imitate the shape of the room—a square design would look awkward in a hallway or a long room.

For both of the examples shown on these pages, follow the layout, setting, and grouting techniques described on *pages 64 to 71*.

BORDER WITH DIAMOND

In this design, squares of mosaic tiles cut in half border a large section of tiles turned to 45 degrees. Half the angled tiles are white, while the other half are either field tiles (the same as the ones around the design section) or full-size mosaic squares.

Standard tiles can be used instead of mosaics as long as you can cut them in half precisely. If you are using mosaics, make sure the squares are the same size as the other tiles. If not, you may need to widen or narrow the grout joints around them in order to make the layout work.

LAYING OUT: Lay out the design section first, then lay out the field tiles that cover the rest of the floor. Note that the full-sized mosaic squares do not abut the mosaic border—if they did, the design would look confusing. Also, plan the layout to avoid very small triangles at the sides.

Draw your design on graph paper, then lay all the full-size, diamond-shaped tiles on the floor in a dry run. Check that they are centered in the room in both directions. Then snap chalk lines indicating the inside of the border tiles. Check the lines for square.

Place some border tiles and field tiles in a dry run to make sure you will not have unsightly narrow tiles where the floor meets the wall. You may have to change the size of the design section to avoid such slivers.

INSTALLING: Think through the order of installation so that you never have to step on newly set tiles. Set one side of border tiles first, then the adjacent field tiles.

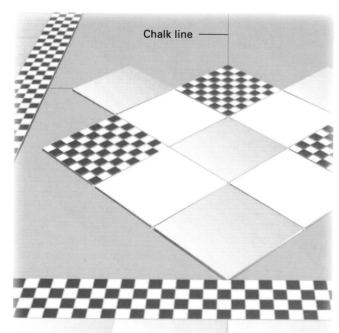

Chalk line

After installing the border tiles, set some interior tiles in a dry run, center them and measure for cut tiles.

Continue setting border and field tiles until most or all of the border is installed.

Next, fill in with the diamond-shaped tiles. Set most of the full tiles in a dry run and check to see that they are all centered, making cut tiles the same size on either side. Cut about a third of the tiles and dry-fit them. When you set the tiles, install the cut ones and full ones at the same time.

CENTER DIAMOND WITH BORDER

This design is easier to lay out and install. However, the four tiles surrounding the center all need to be cut precisely. The border tiles must be exactly half the size of the field tiles. The center tile may be any size you choose; in the design shown, it is the same size as the field tiles.

LAYING OUT: The design is square—the same number of tiles long in each direction. If you choose to make it one or more tiles longer in one direction, you will need to install two new rows of half or full tiles at either end inside the border.

Plan the layout to center the pattern in the room, at least widthwise. If the design will be an odd number of field tiles wide, then the total room must be an odd number of tiles wide or long. If the pattern is an even number long, then the total number of tiles in the room must be even. Lay out as you would for any flooring installation (see *pages 64–67*).

INSTALLING: Start with the field tiles. When you reach the design area, install field tiles about two-thirds of the way around it.

Lay the border tiles on three sides, and mark a line on the floor to show where the fourth side will go. Dry-lay the center diamond-shaped tile in the exact center. Make sure it is at a 45-degree angle to the other tiles, and measure in all four directions.

Cut a cardboard template of the four tiles that will surround the center tile. The template will be the same size as the field tiles, less one corner cut off at 45 degrees. Using spacers, check that it will fit on all four sides. You may need to change the size of the template, or adjust the position of the center tile, or even move the border tiles slightly. Once you have figured the correct size, cut and install the four tiles.

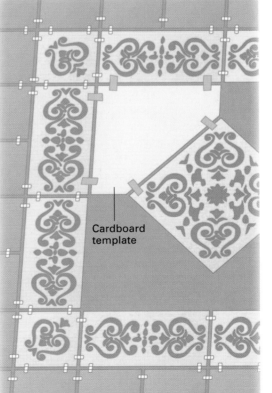

Cardboard template

This design calls for only four pieces to be cut at angles, but those four need to be cut exactly.

It may take several attempts before you make a cardboard template that will fit precisely. Make sure it fits at all four locations.

TILING A COUNTERTOP

A tiled surface resists heat and cleans up easily—ideal qualities for a kitchen countertop. And because tiles come in so many colors, you can design a ceramic top to complement any decor. If you use acrylic- or latex-fortified grout and seal it whenever you notice that water fails to bead, you will have no problems with mildew or cleanup.

sample tile with a metal utensil to make sure it will not scratch easily. In some parts of the country, tile dealers regularly stock field and trim tiles intended for countertops (see *page 29* for some options); in other places, you may have trouble finding all the pieces.

SELECTING MATERIALS

Level the base cabinets in all directions. If necessary, unscrew a cabinet from the wall and shim it up to level it. If two adjoining walls are out of square by more than ½ inch, your tiles may be noticeably misaligned. If possible, take steps to straighten one of the walls.

Make a drawing of the entire job (see box, *page 55*). Take it to your tile retailer or home center for help choosing field tiles, tiles for the front edge and corners, and backsplash materials. In addition, buy grout, spacers, and substrate materials.

SUBSTRATE: The surface underlying the tiles must be strong, flat, and water-resistant. For most countertops, ¾-inch plywood topped with ½-inch cement board will be strong enough. You may be able to lay tile over an existing countertop (see *opposite page*). For a heavily used kitchen or bathroom countertop, lay plastic sheeting to provide a waterproof membrane (see *pages 46–47*).

TILES: Install vitreous or impervious tiles on a countertop. Purchase tiles to trim the front edge, corners, and backsplash. Scrape a

PREPARING THE SUBSTRATE

Check that your countertop is level. Don't make the mistake of sloping it toward the sink—the top and the cabinets will be unattractively misaligned. If you are installing new cabinets, install the first one at the highest point of the floor, and shim carefully so they are level in both directions.

REMOVE AN EXISTING COUNTERTOP: Search underneath and remove all the screws. If the top has been glued with construction adhesive, cut it with a knife. Avoid heavy prying, which could damage the cabinets.

PLYWOOD: Cut and position pieces of ¾-inch plywood for the top, letting them overhang the cabinets by an inch or so. Be careful to cut the edges straight and to square all corners. Level the top, slipping in shims if necessary. Drill pilot holes and attach the top with 2-inch screws driven into the cabinet framing every few inches.

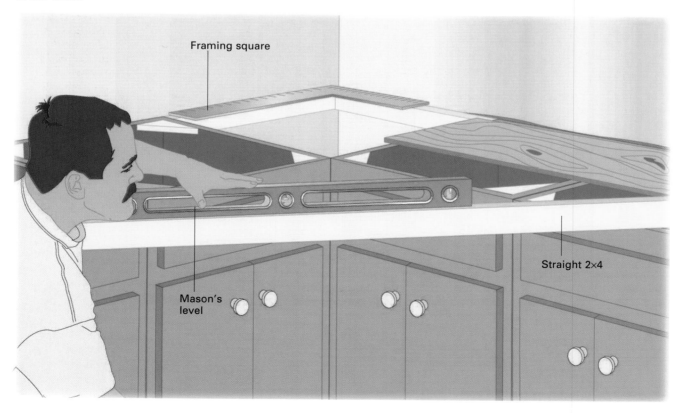

Framing square

Mason's level

Straight 2×4

MEMBRANE: If the top will get wet often, install a waterproofing membrane by laying plastic sheeting in a layer of thin-set mortar (see *pages 46–47*). Place the membrane so it overhangs the front edges an inch and continues up the wall behind the backsplash about 2 inches.

CEMENT BOARD: Cut and dry-fit pieces of cement backerboard, bringing the front edge of each flush with the front edge of the plywood. If you plan to install a radius bullnose for the backsplash, you may need to cut a strip of cement board for backing.

Trowel thin-set over the plywood or the membrane, set the backerboard in it, and attach the backerboard to the plywood with 1¼-inch backerboard screws spaced about 6 inches apart in a grid pattern.

PREPARE FOR THE FRONT EDGE: You can let the edging extend slightly below the bottom edge of the substrate for a cleaner appearance. Don't let tile hang more than ¼ inch below it, however; unsupported tile can be easily cracked off. The backerboard and plywood substrate is 1¼ inches thick.

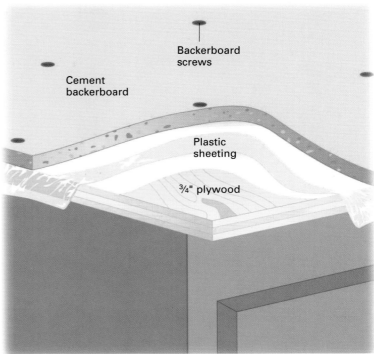

Backerboard screws

Cement backerboard

Plastic sheeting

¾" plywood

After installing a layer of ¾-inch plywood, laminate plastic sheeting between the plywood and the top layer of cement backerboard. For extra waterproofing, use epoxy thin-set instead of latex thin-set.

TILING OVER A LAMINATE COUNTERTOP

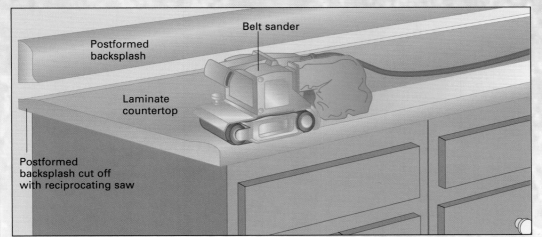

Postformed backsplash

Belt sander

Laminate countertop

Postformed backsplash cut off with reciprocating saw

If you have a laminate countertop that is square, level, and strong, save yourself time and money by installing tiles over it.

If the top has square front edges and a square backsplash, pry off the backsplash. Rough up the surfaces with a hand sander or belt sander and 60- or 80-grit sandpaper.

A postformed top, the kind with a rounded front drip edge and a rounded backsplash (like the one shown *above*), requires more work.

Flatten the top of the front edge with a belt sander or power planer. To remove the backsplash, cut it at the base with a reciprocating saw or a saber saw, angling the cut slightly downward. Make sure the top is flat all across its surface. Rough up the entire surface with a belt sander or hand sander.

Install tiles on the countertop with epoxy thin-set to make sure they will stick.

TILING A COUNTERTOP
continued

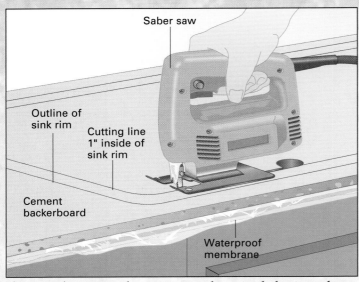

CUTTING A HOLE FOR A SINK

Saber saw

Outline of sink rim

Cutting line 1" inside of sink rim

Cement backerboard

Waterproof membrane

If your sink comes with a cutout template, simply lay it on the top and draw around it, making sure you place it parallel to the front edge of the top. Without a template, set the sink upside down on the top, trace its outline, and draw a parallel line about 1 inch inside the outline. Check the cabinet below to make sure that there are no obstructions, then saw the *inside* line.

Countertop layout can produce some surprises, so make sure you solve all the problems before mixing the mortar. Make a dry run with all the spacers in place. Avoid leaving tile slivers at the ends of the the countertop or around the sink.

If your trim requires a thicker substrate, attach a strip of wood underneath the plywood to bring the edge to the correct thickness. Glue the wood in place, bringing its edge flush with the countertop. Clamp until dry.

CUT A HOLE FOR A SINK: Self-rimming sinks, which rest on top of the tile, are the most common and the easiest to install. A flush-mounted sink sits on top of the substrate, with tiles installed up to its edge. Although harder to install—requiring radius bullnose pieces all around—it makes cleanup easier because there is no lip to trap crumbs.

LAYING OUT THE JOB

You should install the field tiles, front edging, and backsplash at the same time. Before you mix the thin-set, make sure that every piece will fit. Laying out a countertop often requires some compromises, such as placing narrow tiles either near a sink or at one end.

LINE UP THE BULLNOSE OR V-CAP: Begin your layout by positioning the tiles for the edging, such as the bullnose or V-cap. Draw a line with a straightedge or snap a chalk line to indicate the rear edge of the bullnose or V-cap tiles along the front and side edges. Also, mark the edges of the tiles that will abut a flush-mounted sink if you are installing one. After positioning the edges, you can fill in with field tiles.

MAKE A DRY RUN: Place as many tiles as possible on the top, with spacers between them to make sure there will be no surprises when you start laying tile. If the back of the countertop abuts a wall, plan to lay a row of cut tiles against the wall. Symmetrical rows of cut tiles along both edges of an island countertop will probably look better.

FOR A STRAIGHT COUNTERTOP: Mark the centerline of the countertop—or the sink—and lay the tiles out from it so the cut pieces along each edge of the top or beside the sink will be the same width. If this creates narrow slivers, however, adjust the layout to place a single row of larger cut tiles on one side; asymmetrical tiles are preferable to symmetrical slivers.

FOR AN L-SHAPED TOP: If the countertop turns a corner, begin dry-laying field tiles at the inside corner. Set the V-cap or front bullnose tiles in place, ensuring that bullnose pieces overhang the correct amount. You may have to cut two pieces of V-cap or front bullnose at the corner. (See *page 80* for two types of corner pieces.) Make these cuts now.

BATTENS FOR EDGING LAYOUT

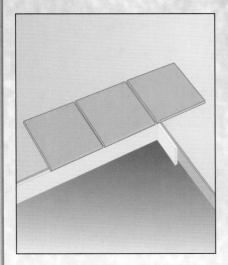

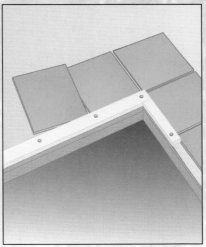

For bullnose tiles (*far left*) tack a wood strip the same thickness as the edging tiles to the countertop edge. Place the bullnose tiles on the top, with their rounded edges flush with the face of the spacing strip to determine the location of the batten, again allowing for a grout line.

For V-cap edging, attach a temporary batten to the top to define the edge of the V-cap, (*left*). Align the field tiles against the batten, then apply the edging in a separate step. Allow for the width of the grout line when positioning the batten.

INSTALLING THE TILES

When you finish the dry run, pick up some or all of the tiles. It usually helps to leave some dry-run tiles in place so you don't have to figure again where to place the tiles as you set them. Lay about 8 square feet of tile at a time. If the countertop is L-shaped, start at the corner and work outward.

ATTACH A BATTEN: If you install a V-cap, temporarily screw a straight piece of 1×2 to the countertop for a batten, or guide. You will set the first row of field tiles against this batten, so position it a grout-joint's width back from the edge of the V-cap to allow a grout line between the cap and the field tiles.

If you will be installing bullnose tiles with edging beneath, the bullnose must overhang the countertop by the thickness of the edging tile. Tack a strip of wood the same thickness as the edging against the counter's edge, then install a batten (see *above*).

MIX AND SPREAD THE THIN-SET: Mix thin-set powder with enough latex additive to give it the consistency of toothpaste. Allow the mixture to slake for 10 minutes or so, then mix again. Add more liquid if necessary. Spread the thin-set over the surface to be tiled, using a trowel with ¼-inch by ¼-inch square notches. First, spread with the straight side of the trowel to press the mortar into the backerboard, then comb with the notched side. Hold the trowel at a consistent 45-degree angle as you work. Scrape away excess blobs of thin-set.

Place the tile to be cut on top of the tile closest to the wall. Place another tile on top of it, two grout-widths away from the wall. Mark for the cut by drawing alongside the top tile.

LAY AND BED THE TILES: Press (don't slide) each tile gently into place, fitting spacers between them to maintain consistent grout joints. Once a section has been laid, tap it with a beater block (see *page 68*) to bed the tiles in the thin-set and level the surface. When fitting the last row against a wall, mark each piece individually (shown *above*) in case the wall is out of square. (See *page 69* for techniques to measure and cut tiles to fit.)

TILING A COUNTERTOP
continued

EDGING INSIDE CORNERS

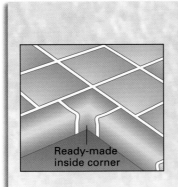

Ready-made inside corner

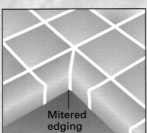

Mitered edging

A ready-made piece is ideal to handle inside corner edging. You won't always be able to find them, however. You can make your own inside corners by miter-cutting straight edging with a wet saw (see *page 53*). Cutting the pieces may allow you to line up grout lines, too.

BACKSPLASH AND EDGING OPTIONS

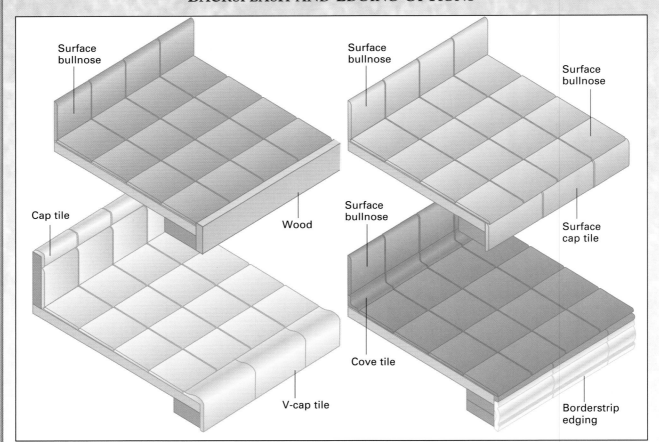

Surface bullnose
Surface bullnose
Surface bullnose
Cap tile
Wood
Surface bullnose
Surface cap tile
V-cap tile
Cove tile
Borderstrip edging

The front edging is one of the most visible elements of a tiled countertop, so choose yours with care. If you decide to use wood edging, seal it well with polyurethane and apply silicone caulk between the tiles and the wood. V-cap lends a unified look to your top, and its shape keeps spilled liquid from running down onto the floor. Borderstrip edging—which rests under bullnose tiles— allows you to add a decorative element.

Most countertop tile edgings are about 1¼ inches deep. Make sure your edging leaves space to open the door, drawer, or dishwasher underneath the top without pinching your fingers.

The three backsplash options above use materials that match the countertop. You can also use different colored tiles or other materials, such as wood or even a piece of marble.

INSTALL EDGING AND BACKSPLASH:
After you have laid all the field tiles, remove
any battens. Then, to install the edging, apply
thin-set to the countertop and silicone
adhesive to its edge. Press the edging pieces
into place, making sure you bring their top
surfaces flush with the other tiles. Work fairly
quickly because the silicone will start to cure
soon after you squeeze it on.

Set the backsplash tiles in silicone as well.
Install them the same way as shown on *page
72* for adding baseboard tiles to a floor.

GROUT AND CLEAN: Allow the mortar to
set completely, which will take at least a day.
Remove the spacers and grout the surface as
you would a tiled floor (see *pages 70 and 71*).
Put sanded grout in joints wider than ¹⁄₁₆ inch.
Mix the grout with latex, not water, for
strength and durability. Try to get the grout
joints nearly flush with the tile surface; deep
grout joints are harder to keep clean on a
countertop. Caulk rather than grout the
joint between the countertop tiles and the
backsplash tiles.

A week or two after grouting, apply grout
sealer for protection against stains and for
easier cleaning.

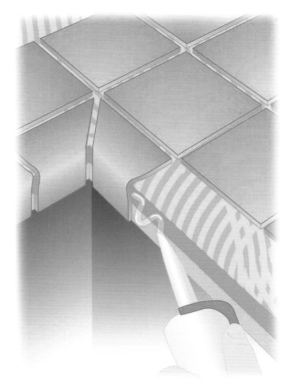

*Attach edging
pieces with
thin-set on the
countertop and
silicone adhesive
(clear silicone
caulk) on the
edges. Attach
a V-cap in the
same way.*

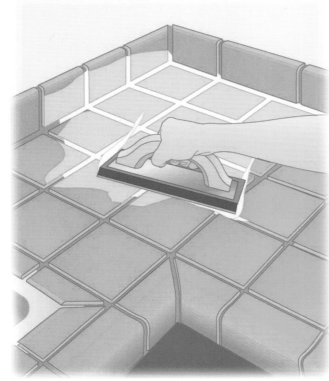

*Hold the grout float nearly flat to press the grout into
the joints. Then wipe away the excess grout by tilting
the float up and using it like a squeegee.*

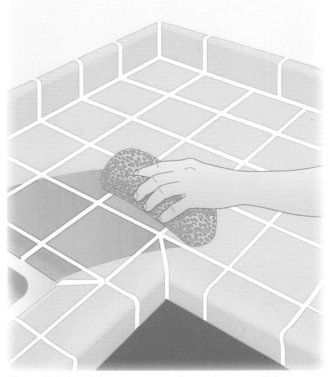

*Press lightly with a sponge to keep the grout joints
nearly flush with the tile surface. Take time to make
these conspicuous grout lines neat.*

WORKING WITH GRANITE AND MARBLE TILE

Natural stone tiles have a subtle beauty unmatched by any other material. They are sometimes difficult to install, but are not out of reach for a motivated do-it-yourselfer. Here's how to work with stone tile.

TILING FLOORS AND WALLS

In general, granite and marble tiles require the same installation techniques as ceramic tile. For instructions on laying out and setting wall tiles, see *pages 54–61*; for floor tiles, see *pages 64–73*. Here are a few points to keep in mind when working with stone tile:

■ Question your tile dealer closely to make sure the tiles you buy will perform as needed. Will they stain or scratch easily? If so, can they be cleaned or repolished? (See *page 26*.)

■ Ask your tile dealer to recommend an adhesive for your tile—usually, standard thin-set or epoxy thin-set. Light-colored marble is somewhat translucent and should be set in slightly more expensive white thin-set. Gray thin-set will show through the marble.

■ Provide a firm, flat substrate for a floor. These tiles crack more easily than standard ceramic tiles.

■ Keep them close. Marble and granite floors and walls look best with thin grout lines, or none at all. Lay the tiles with ⅟₁₆-inch or ⅛-inch spacers, or butt the pieces together.

Make a complete dry run before you start to set tiles. When installing with silicone caulk, lift up only one or two tiles at a time, squirt a random pattern onto the substrate, and immediately place the tile onto the caulk. Make sure adjacent pieces are level with each other.

HANDHELD STONE CUTTERS

To cut granite or marble perfectly straight, rent a wet saw (see *pages 52–53*). But for cuts that will be covered by molding or a sink, you can buy or rent a less-cumbersome electric grinder with a diamond blade. Many professional installers cut granite and marble this way.

You also could buy a handheld wet saw like the one shown above. Use it outdoors; a pair of tubes continually squirt water onto its diamond blade as you work.

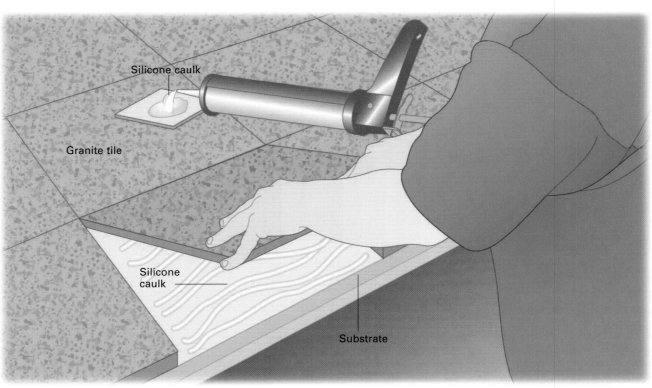

Silicone caulk

Granite tile

Silicone caulk

Substrate

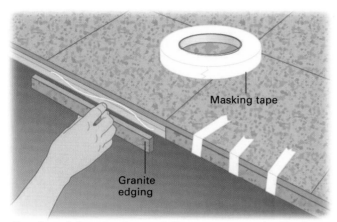

Granite edging that is carefully set presents the illusion of a thick slab of granite. Make sure you line up all the adjacent edges evenly.

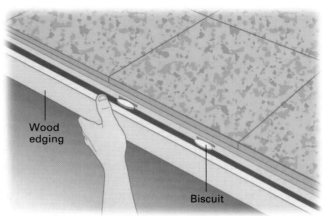

For a wood edge unmarred by fasteners, slot the edging and countertop with a biscuit joiner. Then glue on the edging, aligning it with the football-shaped biscuits.

TILING A COUNTERTOP WITH GRANITE

Few countertops are quite as imposing as a granite slab. It's practical and easy to clean. But it demands costly professional installation. For a fraction of the price, you can cover a countertop with granite tiles and get the same effect. The resulting surface will have subtle joint lines with no grout.

Begin by preparing the countertop substrate as you would for a standard tiled installation (see *pages 76–78*).

CHOOSE AN EDGING: To create the illusion of a thick slab, edge the top with strips of the same granite tile. Cut the strips with a wet saw, making them as wide as the edge. The edges of the first row of surface tiles will be exposed, so have them polished. Install the edging as you set the surface tiles.

To install a hardwood edge, set the tiles flush with the front edge. After the adhesive has set, attach the hardwood edging (1×2 pieces work well). For easy cleaning, attach the top edge of the edging about ¹⁄₁₆ inch lower than the tile surface. Attach it with finish nails or trimhead screws and glue, drilling pilot holes first. Or use a biscuit joiner (see *above right*) for edging that's free of fastener holes.

MAKE A DRY RUN: Lay every tile in place—including the cut tiles—before you begin installing them. Dry-test your edging pieces to make sure you will have tight, straight joints. If the backsplash will be tile, cut and test-fit those pieces as well.

INSTALL THE TILES: Ask your tile dealer to recommend the best adhesive for your particular granite. Professionals often set these tiles in clear silicone adhesive/caulk. If you use that, do a careful dry run and work fast—the silicone sets up pretty quickly. Or you can set the tiles in epoxy thin-set.

ROUND AND POLISH AN EDGING

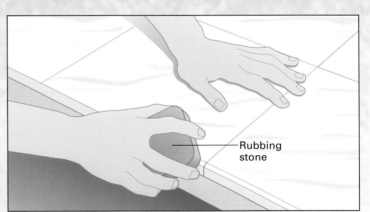

Round off sharp corners with a rubbing stone. The stone can also shape an edge of soft marble. If the edge of a marble or granite tile will be exposed, it should be polished to a shine similar to the finished surface of the tiles. For highly visible spots like the edge of a countertop, ask your tile dealer to recommend a professional who can polish the edges for you. If the edge will not be noticeable—for example, the edge of a floor tile—rub the edge with a rubbing stone or with fine sandpaper, and brush on several coats of clear lacquer.

Press the tiles gently into the adhesive. Pick up tiles occasionally to make sure that the adhesive is sticking uniformly. Bed the tiles and level the surface with a beater block (see *pages 68–69*). Install granite edging strips as you go, or test pieces of wood edging to make sure they will fit securely to the granite.

SEAL: There is no need for grout. After the adhesive has dried, apply a sealer made for granite and marble to the entire top. Several coats may be needed to fill the joints.

TILING AROUND A FIREPLACE

For a small investment in time and materials, you can turn a tired-looking fireplace into a fabulous focal point. Not only does tile look great on a hearth or fireplace surround, it also provides a durable, noncombustible surface.

While you're working with the fireplace, have it and the chimney safety-inspected. (Do this once a year.) Repair any damage before you light another fire. You also may need a chimney cleaning to remove creosote, which can cause a dangerous chimney fire.

TILING A HEARTH

Local building codes specify how far non-combustible materials must extend out from and to the sides of the fireplace opening, as well as which materials are recommended.

Usually, tiles set in thin-set on top of a sheet of ½-inch cement backerboard will suffice. The hearth in an older home may be smaller than current codes require, so it would have to be enlarged before tiling.

Hearth tiles don't have to reach all the way to the back of the fireplace, but tiling that extends into it at least 1 foot looks best.

PREPARING FOR A NEW HEARTH: If the existing hearth is cracked but strong, you can tile over it. (To tile over an existing tile surface, see *page 38*.) That will raise the height of the hearth, but you can trim the edges with bullnose tile or hardwood molding.

If the existing tile is loose, chip it away with a hammer and cold chisel. The substrate in older homes may be concrete; make sure it is firm before tiling over it (see *page 36*). If the surface is firm but uneven, mix some latex-fortified thin-set and smooth it on as a skim coat, using the flat edge of a trowel.

Plan the job to use as few cut tiles as possible. Narrow cut pieces usually do not look attractive on a hearth.

EXTENDING A RAISED HEARTH: The hearth may stand 2 inches or so higher than the floor in an older home. It might be smaller than codes call for, too. To enlarge a raised hearth, build a substrate of 2-by lumber covered with cement backerboard (see *below*). Start by rip-cutting pieces of 2×4 or 2×2 to a width 1 inch less than the hearth's height. Attach one piece to the hearth edge with screws into anchors or with masonry screws. Attach the other pieces to the floor and to each other with screws. To provide firm support, members should be no more than 12 inches apart at any point. Cover the wood frame with two thicknesses of backerboard (see *pages 44 and 45*).

If the hearth will be raised above floor level, cover its edges with attractive wood molding. The floor should be firm so that tiles won't crack if a log gets dropped on them.

Wood molding

Hearth tile

A small hearth may result in sparks damaging your flooring or carpeting. To extend a raised hearth, build a frame with 2-by lumber and cover it with cement backerboard.

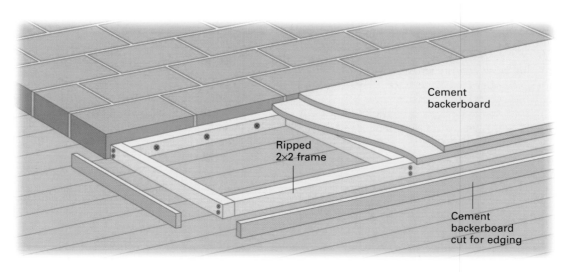

Cement backerboard

Ripped 2×2 frame

Cement backerboard cut for edging

SETTING THE TILES: Follow standard floor-tiling techniques (see *pages 64–71*) to set and grout the tiles. Install bullnose tile edging or hardwood edging at the same time you set the tile. (Cover hardwood edging with masking tape before grouting to avoid damaging it.)

TILING A FIREPLACE SURROUND

You can apply wall tiles directly over walls surrounding the fireplace, as long as each wall is structurally sound and heat-resistant. Install the wall tiles as described on *pages 54–59*, but set them in heat-resistant thin-set mortar rather than organic mastic.

TILING UP TO A MANTEL: You may be able to remove a molding beneath the mantel, install the tiles, then reinstall the molding to cover the tile edges. Or perhaps you could add a molding under the mantel. Otherwise, simply tile up to the mantel and caulk the joint.

LAYING OUT: If the edges of your wall tiles aren't finished, cover them with a row of bullnose pieces placed on the inside edges of the fireplace opening. Of course, you shouldn't cover the inside edge of a fireplace surround with wood molding.

As with the hearth, plan to cut as few tiles as possible. If the tiles you want cannot be installed without narrow slivers, consider a different-size tile or different spacing.

PREPARING THE SURFACES: If you will be installing tile on the wall as well as inside the fireplace opening, you may need to straighten one of the surfaces so the tiles can fit together snugly and evenly. Test-fit all the pieces to make sure they will form straight rows. If necessary, spread on a skim coat of heat-resistant thin-set with the straight edge of a trowel to produce a smooth surface. Allow it to set before applying more thin-set and installing the tiles.

SETTING THE TILES: Start by installing the bullnose edging across the top edge of the fireplace opening. Place them so they extend beyond the face of the fireplace by the thickness of a tile. Mix and apply thin-set or epoxy adhesive with a notched trowel, and set the tiles in it. Bed the tiles with a beater block. Using 1×4 uprights, prop a straight 2×4 batten to hold the edging in place (see *above*).

Install the vertical pieces of bullnose and then the field tiles. Make sure the edges meet evenly. Allow the adhesive to dry before removing the batten. After the adhesive has set (allow about a day), grout the joints and wipe the tiles clean (see *pages 58 and 59*).

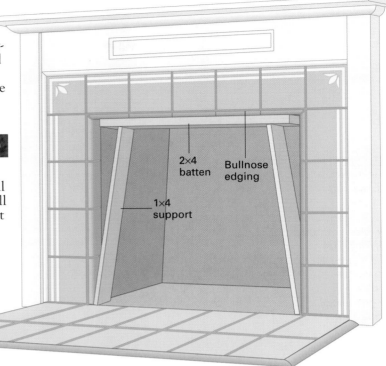

Support the bullnose edging under the top edge of the fireplace opening with a 2×4 batten. Leave in place until the thin-set or epoxy has set.

TOTAL TILE

Decorative tile can transform an unattractive masonry fireplace into an eye-catching centerpiece. Prepare the surface by knocking down any high spots with a belt sander with a 40- or 60-grit belt. Apply a skim coat of thin-set mortar to fill in the mortar lines and smooth out any irregularities.

Plan the layout carefully. Start with the tiles just below the mantel and those just above the fireplace opening, then fill in the spaces between. If you find you'll have to use unattractively narrow pieces, you may be able to solve the problem by increasing the spacing between tiles or by choosing tiles of a different size.

TILING AN OUTDOOR SURFACE

Outdoor tiles or pavers can quickly transform an old concrete slab or stairway. After you've prepared the surface and chosen an edging style, outdoor tiling is much like an indoor installation.

PREPARE A CONCRETE SLAB

Outdoor tile should usually be installed on a solid concrete slab—one that is free of large cracks and that feels firm at all points. It should slope away from the house so that no puddles form on it after a rainfall. If a slab has a crack that grows from year to year, tiles installed on it will probably crack, too.

A NEW SLAB: If you have no concrete pad, have a contractor lay one at least 3 inches thick, resting on a bed of well-tamped gravel. For extra strength, have wire reinforcing mesh embedded in the slab.

REPAIRING A SLAB: For how to inspect and repair a concrete surface, see *page 36.* To repair a cracked edge, chisel away all loose material, then paint the area with a latex bonding agent. Make a simple form by placing a board up against the edge and holding it in place with heavy bricks or blocks. Fill the space between the form and the slab with patching concrete, and trowel smooth.

CLEAN OR ROUGH UP THE SURFACE: Outdoor surfaces often are coated with oil or grease, which will make it difficult for tiles to stick. Clean the slab with a stiff brush and a solution of water and detergent. Or rent a power washer and blast away the grime.

Thin-set may not adhere well if the surface is very smooth. Rent a grinding tool to roughen smooth concrete.

APPLY ISOLATION MEMBRANE: Spread trowel-applied isolation membrane to the entire surface to reduce the risk of cracked tiles. Apply first with the notched side of a trowel, then smooth the surface with the smooth edge. (See *pages 46 and 47.*)

A trowel-applied membrane will keep cracks in the slab from transferring to the tiles above.

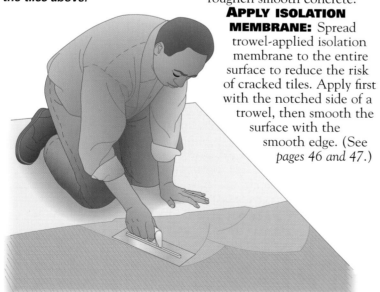

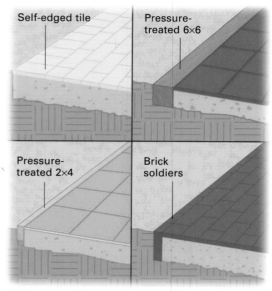

Edging provides some protection, but is mostly cosmetic. The simplest approach is to make the tile the edge. With a bit of digging you can stake in place some wood edging or install upright brick soldiers.

Self-edged tile

Pressure-treated 6×6

Pressure-treated 2×4

Brick soldiers

INSTALL EDGING

A tiled patio or walk usually needs edging, for the sake of appearance as well as to protect tile edges from damage. Four edging options are shown above.

If you edge with wood, use lumber that resists rot, such as pressure-treated material or redwood. Set upright brick soldiers in a bed of sand, using a string line to make sure they stay straight and level. When paving with thicker materials, such as brick, you may decide to edge with a simple row of flat-laid pavers.

In most cases, you should install the edging first, then lay the tile. If your slab is slightly out of square (see *page 64*), you may be able to compensate by installing the edging in such a way that a few of the tiles slightly overhang the concrete. This will make the tiled surface look square.

Most edgings are installed by first digging a trench around the perimeter. Because slabs are not perfectly laid, you may need to chip away concrete with a hammer and cold chisel. If you need to remove a large amount, cut it away with a rented masonry saw to avoid cracking the slab.

To allow water to drain away from the boards, shovel gravel into the trench and tamp it well. Brick soldiers can be set directly in the soil. Use a string line or a level to keep

To pave a concrete slab, spread a thick layer of mason's mortar with a long, straight board called a screed. Space the tiles with pieces of plywood. Wait a day, then grout the joints with more mortar.

your edging straight. The edging should slope away from the house by about ¼ inch per foot.

SET THE TILES

Use the techniques for setting and grouting floor tiles described on *pages 64–71*. Apply caulk instead of grout where the tiles meet the house. Do not apply caulk or grout where tiles meet wood edging so water can freely seep down and away.

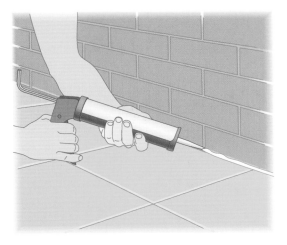

The house and patio will expand and contract in different ways, so apply flexible caulk, not grout, to the joint where they meet.

TILING A STAIRWAY

To tile over concrete stairs, place bullnose pieces like these at the front of the treads, or purchase edging tiles similar to V-caps for countertops. Mixing in a few decorative tiles can make a dramatic difference.

THE RIGHT MATERIALS

If winter brings freezing weather in your area, select vitreous or impervious tiles that are known to be durable in your climate. Nonvitreous pavers are popular in warm climates. Unglazed tiles usually are the best choice because they cut the sun's glare and provide a slip-resistant surface when wet.

In areas that have cold winters, use a concrete patching material and an adhesive that can withstand freezing (they will be labeled "freeze/thaw stable").

If your grout cracks or begins to crumble, remove as much as you can with a grout saw or reamer (below). Weak grout comes out easily; if grout is difficult to saw out, it is structurally sound. After removing the old, apply new grout, using the techniques described on pages 58 and 59.

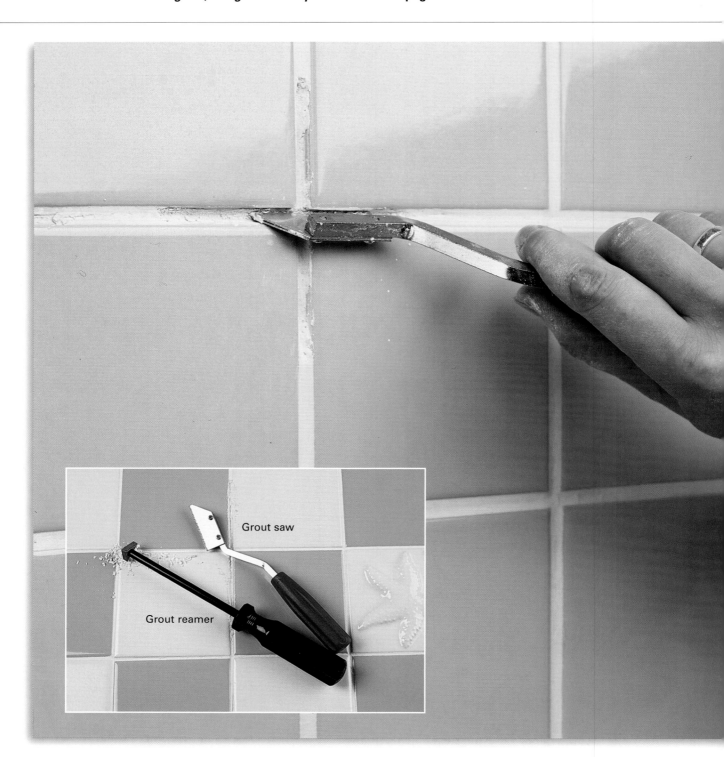

Grout saw

Grout reamer

REPAIRS & MAINTENANCE

Ceramic tile is usually durable and easy to keep clean. Installed correctly, it should last for many decades before it needs repair.

Occasionally, a tile may break if a heavy object hits it. Once you find a replacement of the same size and color, installing a new tile should take only an hour or two.

Structural problems often cause tile failures. Old floors and walls may sag or shift, cracking tile or grout. But, you could choose to live with a minor crack or two, accepting it as part of the charm of an older home. If the surface gets wet regularly, you can seal the cracks with grout or caulk to prevent water damage to the substrate and surrounding grout.

Problems may also occur because the tile wasn't installed properly. The substrate may not be firm, the adhesive may not be strong enough, or the grout may have been mixed with water only and no latex additive.

Poor materials are sometimes at fault. If a large area of a tile surface has become worn-looking and cleaning does not bring back the luster, the tiles themselves may have had a weak glaze. The only solution is to remove them and install new tiles.

Grout can be removed and reinstalled in a day, but any of the other problems will require removing the tiles and starting over again. If grout has become dingy, or if unglazed tiles or natural stone tiles have become stained, this section will show you how to restore them to their original beauty.

CLEANING AND REMOVING STAINS

A tiled surface is easy to keep in pristine condition: Clean it regularly and apply sealer occasionally, and you won't have to face stubborn stains. To keep it clean, wipe ceramic tile and grout regularly with a household cleaner or weak solution of water and dishwashing liquid. Keep tile floors swept so hard particles won't be ground into grout joints.

SEALING GROUT: If a tile surface often gets wet, apply grout sealer after cleaning the surface thoroughly. Apply sealer with a special applicator or a small sponge paintbrush. Sealers usually last a year or two. If water does not bead up on your grout joints, it's time for another application of sealer.

SEALING UNGLAZED TILES: Quarry tiles, unglazed pavers, and natural stone tiles will absorb moisture and stains if not sealed. Purchase a sealer designed for use on your tiles from a tile dealer, and apply it with a sponge or a paint roller. Water should bead up on the tile instead of soaking in; if not, apply another coat of sealer.

REMOVING STAINS: The general rule for removing stains is to first try the mildest cleaner, then proceed to harsher products as necessary. The chart below lists solutions for some specific cleaning problems.

CLEANING GROUT HAZE: After applying grout and wiping the tiles with a damp sponge twice, you can usually just use a dry cloth to buff away the haze that forms on the tiles. The haze may occasionally be difficult to remove, especially if the tiles are unglazed. Try household cleaners first. If they don't work, contact your tile dealer for a product that will remove the grout haze without damaging your type of tile.

ACID CLEANING FOR TOUGH PROBLEMS: If a stain is so stubborn that nothing else will remove it, you may have to resort to an acid-based heavy-duty cleaner, available from tile dealers. Wear protective gloves, goggles, and a dust mask for this job, and keep the room well ventilated to reduce fumes. Mix and apply the cleaner in accordance with the manufacturer's instructions. Scrub vigorously with a scrubbing pad that has a handle. (Don't scrub with a brush; that will spatter the acid all over the room.) Rinse two or three times.

GROUT COLORANT

A grout colorant can cover stains on grout as well as give the tile surface a new look—some colorant can even change grout from a dark color to a lighter one. To apply colorant, first clean the grout thoroughly. Paint on the colorant (it usually comes with an applicator brush), and allow it to soak in for about 10 minutes. Wipe away the excess, and let it dry. Apply a second coat if necessary.

STAIN-CLEANING CHART

Stain	Cleaning Agent
Cooking grease and fat	Wipe or brush with a strong solution of household cleaner or floor cleaner.
Blood and food products like grape juice, wine, coffee, and tea	Rub a paste of baking soda and water onto the stain, allow to dry, and wipe off. If that doesn't work, wipe with full-strength bleach. If the stain still remains, ask your tile dealer to recommend a heavy-duty cleaner.
Dried paint	Scrub with a product designed to clean off dried latex paint. Or brush on paint remover, let sit for 10 minutes, then wipe away.
Rust or white-colored mineral deposits	Brush with a product specifically designed to clean rust or lime deposits, then rinse thoroughly.

ADDING ACCESSORIES

You don't have to remove tiles to install a soap dish, toothbrush holder, or other accessories. Many are designed to install directly on top of ceramic tile. For amenities like shower doors or curtain rods, you may need to drill holes through tiles.

ATTACHING AN ACCESSORY WITH ADHESIVE: Regular organic mastic generally isn't strong enough to hold glue-on items; an epoxy adhesive is better. Ask your tile dealer to recommend an adhesive.

Rough up the tile surface with sandpaper or a rubbing stone where you will be attaching the accessory. Spread adhesive on the tile and on the back of the accessory. Press the accessory into place, then remove it and allow the adhesive to dry for a few minutes. Press the accessory back into place, and wipe away any excess. Hold the accessory in place with strips of masking tape (*above right*).

Do not touch the accessory for at least a day; for best results, wait several days to allow the adhesive to fully harden. Remove the tape and caulk around the accessory so water won't seep in.

DRILLING A HOLE: You can drill a hole less than ¾ inch in diameter with a masonry drill bit. But for best results, try a bit designed specifically to bore through ceramic tile.

To start a hole with either bit, first lightly chip the glaze with a sharp nail and hammer to keep the bit from slipping off the mark as you drill. Apply a few drops of oil to the hole to keep from dulling the bit. Press firmly as you drill, but don't push down too hard or you might crack the tile.

Don't overheat the bit when drilling through tough floor tile or concrete. Spray the hole and the bit with window cleaner as you work (see *center right*). This will cool the bit and help bring grit out of the hole.

Use a carbide-tipped hole saw to bore a precise hole larger than ¾ inch in diameter. Press lightly when you drill so you won't crack the tile. If the hole does not need to be exact, drill a series of holes around its edge and knock out the middle.

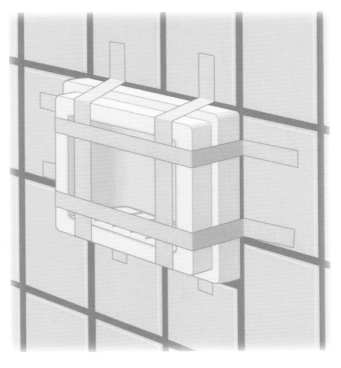

Tell family members not to touch an accessory that has been glued to a tile surface for a day or two so the adhesive can achieve full strength.

Tile-cutting bit

When using a tile-cutting bit, spray the hole with glass cleaner to cool the blade and to foam the grit out of the hole.

Several types of bits can cut through tile. Dense floor tiles are more difficult to drill through than wall tiles.

REPLACING DAMAGED TILE AND GROUT

A damaged tile surface might need just a simple repair and some cleaning to look fresh and new again. If tiles are buckling or even popping out from a wall or floor, you'll have to find out why before you can repair it.

ADHESIVE PROBLEMS: If the tiles come off by themselves, leaving a solid surface underneath, then the thin-set or mastic has failed, perhaps because it was not strong enough in the first place. (See *page 49* for how to choose the correct adhesive.)

Remove all the loose tiles. Scrape the adhesive off the tile backs and the substrate; a paint scraper usually works well for this. Set the tiles back in place to make sure they will all rest flat. Then reapply the tiles, setting them in organic mastic or thin-set.

SUBSTRATE PROBLEMS: If part of the wall or floor is stuck to the tile when you pull it off or if the substrate is weak and crumbling, you have a larger job on your hands. Water has probably seeped in and damaged the surface behind the tiles.

In this case, remove all the loose tiles. If it's too difficult to scrape the old adhesive off the tiles, find replacement tiles that match. Remove the damaged

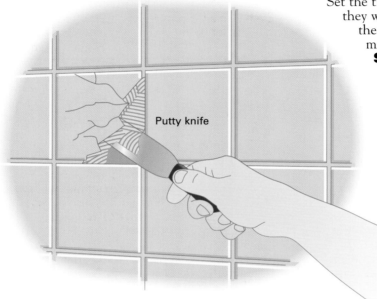

To avoid damage to surrounding tiles, work from the center outward. Pry gently when removing a cracked tile.

Putty knife

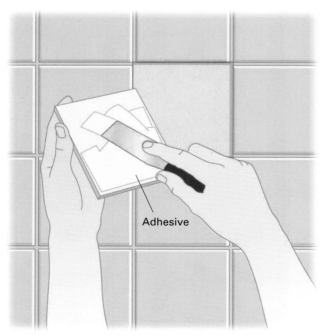

Adhesive

Butter the back of the replacement tile with plenty of adhesive. Press the tile into place, and clean away any adhesive that squeezes out the sides.

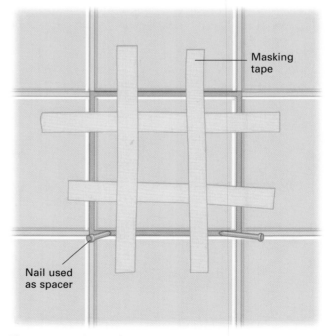

Masking tape

Nail used as spacer

If necessary, insert finishing nails as spacers when installing a replacement wall tile. Masking tape will hold the tile in place and remind others not to touch the tile.

substrate all the way to the next joist or stud. Add nailers to the studs if necessary. Replace the damaged substrate with cement backer-board to provide a solid, even surface before you retile and regrout. (You may need to build up the area with plywood first.)

BROKEN TILES

Ceramic tiles may crack if they are not strong enough for their use, if the underlying structure is not rigid enough, or if they have been subjected to extreme force.

WEAK TILES: If several tiles have cracked even though nothing heavy was dropped on them, the tiles may be too weak for the job. For instance, wall tiles may have been installed on a floor. If this is the case, don't wait for more damage to occur; redo the entire installation with stronger tile.

WEAK STRUCTURE: If a floor flexes noticeably when you jump on it, tiles may be cracking due to the weak underlying structure. Strengthen the framing from below if you can. Otherwise, you will need to remove the tiles and substrate and rebuild the floor before retiling (see *pages 34–36*).

CRACKED TILE: If only one or two tiles have been damaged and the structure is sound, you need only remove the damaged tiles. If the cracked pieces do not pull out

easily, chip them away with a hammer and cold chisel. Tap lightly to avoid damaging adjacent tiles. Remove the grout, and smooth the substrate. Butter a replacement tile with adhesive, and press it into place. You may need to slip in some spacers—often nails will do. Wait a day or two before grouting.

REGROUTING

Even a small gap in an area that often gets wet can let in enough water to damage the substrate. If you have only a few gaps in grout that is otherwise sound, simply fill them in with latex-reinforced grout of the same color.

If you don't like the color of your grout or if the color is uneven, try recoloring it (see box on *page 90*). If the grout is cracked or flaking in many places, it's time to regrout.

To regrout, first remove the old grout with a grout saw or grout reamer (see *page 88*). Try not to rush this tedious job; it's easy to damage nearby tiles. After removing the damaged grout, vacuum up the dust. Scrub the entire surface with tile cleaner to eliminate oils and soap scum, which can inhibit the ability of the new grout to hold.

Apply the grout as you would on a new installation (see *pages 58, 59, 70, and 71*). Caulk joints where the tile abuts a fixture or another surface (see *page 59*).

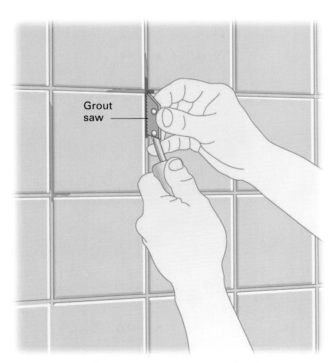

Grout saw

Saw with steady, even pressure when working with a grout saw. Work carefully to avoid damaging tiles.

Fill in occasional small gaps in grout, using that most flexible of tools, your finger.

INDEX

METRIC CONVERSIONS

U.S. Units to Metric Equivalents			Metric Units to U.S. Equivalents		
To Convert From	Multiply By	To Get	To Convert From	Multiply By	To Get
Inches	25.4	Millimeters	Millimeters	0.0394	Inches
Inches	2.54	Centimeters	Centimeters	0.3937	Inches
Feet	30.48	Centimeters	Centimeters	0.0328	Feet
Feet	0.3048	Meters	Meters	3.2808	Feet
Yards	0.9144	Meters	Meters	1.0936	Yards
Square inches	6.4516	Square centimeters	Square centimeters	0.1550	Square inches
Square feet	0.0929	Square meters	Square meters	10.764	Square feet
Square yards	0.8361	Square meters	Square meters	1.1960	Square yards
Acres	0.4047	Hectares	Hectares	2.4711	Acres
Cubic inches	16.387	Cubic centimeters	Cubic centimeters	0.0610	Cubic inches
Cubic feet	0.0283	Cubic meters	Cubic meters	35.315	Cubic feet
Cubic feet	28.316	Liters	Liters	0.0353	Cubic feet
Cubic yards	0.7646	Cubic meters	Cubic meters	1.308	Cubic yards
Cubic yards	764.55	Liters	Liters	0.0013	Cubic yards

To convert from degrees Fahrenheit (F) to degrees Celsius (C), first subtract 32, then multiply by ⅝.

To convert from degrees Celsius to degrees Fahrenheit, multiply by ⅝, then add 32.